FLOWER
AND
GARDEN
PHOTOGRAPHY

*Dedicated to my parents, for
all the time and for everything—
without them . . . nothing.*

FLOWER
AND
GARDEN
PHOTOGRAPHY

by D.X. FENTEN

AMPHOTO **American Photographic Book Publishing Co., Inc.**
New York

Contents

Preface

The trees are all mulched and wrapped against the drying effects of winter. The gladiolus bulbs have been dug and put away for next year. The roses are mounded and protected. The chrysanthemums are fast fading.

Now, as we enter into the long winter season, we realize how much we miss the flowers, the flowering shrubs, and the green-leafed trees. It will be a long, long time before nature sheds its winter mantle and starts to bloom again. But there is one saving grace—the photos taken all during the spring, summer, and fall. While we cannot touch the velvety smoothness of a rose, marvel at gladiolus florets opening, or taste the magnificence of home-grown corn, tomatoes, and cantaloupes, we can do the next best thing—see them again in photos. These are the photos that will help to warm us until the sun again takes over.

We sincerely hope this book will give many gardeners the information they need so they will be able to keep warm in the glow of photographs taken when nature was at its peak. We also hope this book will entice many photographers into gardening as a hobby and a source for magnificent photographic subjects. Whatever the impact of this book, we have had triple enjoyment—gardening, photographing, and writing.

The author gratefully acknowledges the photos, information, and suggestions so generously contributed by the leading horticulturists, commercial growers, and photographic manufacturers and suppliers. Special thanks are due my family, friends, and associates, who understand my recluse-like behavior when I say, "I'm writing another book."

To Donna and Jeff go my love for bringing huge quantities of sunshine into my life every day.

To my wife, Barbara, little can be added to what has been said before—eternal thanks and love for everything, which once again includes editing and typing assistance.

November, 1965   D. X. FENTEN

Ferry Morse, sky blue flax

CHAPTER I

Introduction

The exquisite, short-lived beauty of nature asks little in exchange for its offer of complete enjoyment. The problem is preservation. How can anyone capture and record this beauty so it may be viewed, reviewed, and enjoyed again and again?

Photography provides the means for maintaining, for long periods of time, much of the magic that makes nature fascinating—the miracle of growth from seed to flower, the bounty of luscious home-grown vegetables, the colorful catalogue of horticultural experiments, and the resultant triumphs or fiascos. But there is considerably more, for photography is much better than memory, and it's in color, too.

Since few of us are blessed with total recall and most memories become clouded with time, both on a positive and negative level, memory leaves much to be desired in retaining natural beauty. It should then become obvious that for accuracy and repeated enjoyment of actual beauty, rather than a many-times-warmed-over and diluted recollection, the camera is the thing. And it is photography that enables all of us, the horticulturist, the casual gardener, the flower lover, and the photographer, to capture, record, and preserve the beauty that is nature.

Unfortunately, or perhaps fortunately, there is a bit more to flower and garden photography than merely aiming a camera at a flower and pushing a button. For unless photos are taken correctly and come out well, the entire experience can be extremely frustrating and downright disappointing.

It therefore becomes imperative for the flower photographer to learn all he can about his subjects and his equipment. If his interest is casual, most of the necessary information can come slowly but surely through the old, tried-and-true trial-and-error system. However, as I'm sure we have all learned by now, this can be most costly in both money and good shots lost, as well as in patience and enthusiasm. If the gardener or horticulturist really wants good nature photos, he must first learn the fundamentals of good photography and then, and only then, apply these to his subject specialty. An intelligent knowledge of his subject, as well as any of its peculiarities and growing habits, will also stand him in very good stead during his pursuit of good nature shots.

Along with the pooling of information between photography and gardening, there should be the desire to take advantage of every opportunity to get good flower and garden pictures. This means that a camera should become an integral part of your gardening equipment, and that an alert eye for the exquisite beauty of nature automatically should go along with your camera on every outing. It is very often done, and yet still very surprising, to see people so intent on snapping a picture of Aunt Fanny, standing stiff and staring straight into the lens, that they never notice the far prettier picture in the background. Photography's basic rules will tell you never to photograph anyone just standing and staring into the camera. And I

hope that by the time you finish reading this book, your new automatic, alert, beauty-conscious eye will show you the right way to combine the two—funny-faced Fanny and the beautiful background.

This should indicate to both the gardener and the photographer the almost unlimited opportunities for finding and filming the endless bits and pieces of nature's beauty. For wherever one goes, something grows. From the pots of flowers in the seemingly cold cities to the wild flowers along country roads, to the golden fields of rippling wheat, to the cultivated truck gardens, to the flower shows and exhibitions, to the botanical gardens, there is always ample opportunity for nature photography.

So, you see, anyone who is interested in maintaining, for a wide variety of reasons, some of the beauty that is nature, has only to look —to SEE—and to record it on film for future joy.

Butterfly was not disturbed on daffodil because telephoto lens allowed extreme close-up with photographer at a distance.

Malak. Comparative sizes of Batalinii tulip and "normal" tulip against a man's hand.

CHAPTER II

Photography's Garden Tools

The best camera for flower photography is probably the camera you now own and know. Of course, a more expensive, more sophisticated camera would be nice to have, and would probably allow more convenience and latitude in picture taking. But few can argue with the professionals, the vast majority of whom feel that the best photos come from a camera that is an old friend, one that has been used many times under widely varying conditions.

Because all good photographs are the result of a team effort, the team of camera and photographer, it is very important that the photographer know all there is to know about his equipment. However, the fact that the camera you have and therefore know is the one most likely to be used does not preclude an investigation into newer or later model equipment. The decision to buy new or additional equipment should be based on the type of work you plan for the future. Above all, the flower photographer, like all photographers, must realize the importance of this team effort—the finest equipment used by a poor photographer will usually result in work less satisfactory than that produced by a fine photographer using poor equipment.

There are several things to look for when you are deciding whether a new camera is needed or your old one will do the job. These criteria are narrowed considerably for flower and garden photography. For example:

(1) *The viewfinder*—The viewfinders on most cameras provide enough light, and extreme brightness in the viewfinder is not critical. Of course, the more light, the better.

(2) *Composing*—Will your camera pose the problem of parallax compensation, possibly causing you to accidentally lop off part of your flower? Since most flower shots are close-ups, this is very important.

(3) *Film size*—Although sharp 35mm negs can be blown up to 11 X 14 and single-frame negs to 8 X 10 with no problem, the fact is that many flower photographs require cropping to improve composition and provide drama. The thought should be: The bigger the negative, the better.

(4) *Accessories*—The availability of accessories is important in that lenses, filters, etc., make a camera into a complete photographic system, giving great versatility and flexibility to the photographer.

(5) *Exposure*—Automatic or not automatic, that is the question. The best bet here is an automatic or semiautomatic with an override to full manual control. This gives the photographer the option and covers every picture-taking possibility.

(6) *Miscellaneous*—Other obvious things to check out in your present camera or the one you intend to buy include bulkiness, ease of handling, type and ease of film loading, and general picture-taking convenience.

From the simplest, most basic box cameras to the highly gadgeted single-lens reflexes there is, of course, a considerable gap in equipment quality, reliability, and versatility, to say nothing of price! The descriptions that follow are meant to present the garden or flower photographer with capsulized information detailing the advantages and disadvantages of the various camera types. Armed with this information, the photographer should be able either to get better photos with his present camera or be steered in the dirction of new equipment better suited to doing the job.

SINGLE-LENS REFLEX CAMERAS

The best flower photos are close-ups, and the best camera for close-ups is the single-lens reflex. Although the SLR is not a perfect camera, the unique advantage of being able to record on film *exactly* what you see in the groundglass viewer far outweighs any disadvantages or limitations. Because the same lens is used for both viewing and recording the image, there is no chance of losing part of your photo because of parallax. Briefly, and in the simplest terms, the SLR cameras reflect the image as seen by the lens upward, by means of a mirror, onto a groundglass. At this point a prism receives the image from the mirror and aims it into the eyepiece. What you then see in the eyepiece is an enlarged, but exact, replica of the area and perspective that will be recorded on the film when you trip the shutter. As a result, no matter what lens you are using at the time, "normal," wide-angle, or telephoto, you will still see exactly what you will get. With groundglass focusing, by carefully moving the lens back and forth the photographer has the ability to determine photo sharpness while he is still able to do something about it—before tripping the shutter, not after the film has been developed.

Nikon F Photomic T Single Lens Reflex

Leica M3 rangefinder camera with coupled exposure meter

All other viewing systems, except the reflex, give a constant, bright image in the viewfinder. Because the SLR uses the picture-taking lens as a viewfinder, you can see the areas of sharpness and fuzziness in your photo as you compose. This is especially important to the flower photographer shooting a group of flowers, for this feature allows careful, sharp focusing on a single bloom, and the fading of the others into the background.

Naturally, in this case as in all others, there are disadvantages as well as advantages. The chief disadvantage of the SLR is that it is substantially more bulky than many of the rangefinder cameras. Also, there is a bit of a viewing handicap when it is used in dim light, and there is the possibility of focusing problems with the split-image viewfinder as opposed to the double-image type found on most other cameras. However, the statement made earlier bears repating: These disadvantages are more than overcome by the ability of the photographer to see exactly what he is getting, no matter what lens is being used.

RANGEFINDER (35mm) CAMERAS

Rangefinder cameras (also called miniature and 35mm cameras) are fast-operating, compact, sharp-focusing, and the optimum for candid photography. These advantages, many as they are, offer little to the flower and garden photographer. Actually these particular advantages are relatively unimportant to the flower photographer, and he should carefully assess the disadvantages of this camera.

15

As mentioned, the SLR's are the only cameras that completely eliminate the parallax problem—just about the biggest headache for the close-up photographer. With the rangefinder cameras, especially with close-ups, the danger of lopping off an important part of the photo is ever present. The advantage (for candid photography) of ultrashort-focal-length lenses and the resultant fantastic depth of field becomes a disadvantage to the photographer trying to fade out a background full of flowers around a single bloom. Also, only after the print has been developed (35mm camera) can the photographer actually see the extent of his depth of field sharpness, while with the SLR he sees this sharpness, or lack of it, as he takes the picture.

On the plus side, the rangefinder cameras offer more positive, critical-point focusing, and relative ease of focusing in dim light, as compared with the SLR cameras. Although they are not ideal for flower photography, the rangefinder cameras can be used for this type of work (many of the photos in this book were shot with a Nikon S-2) if the photographer is well enough acquainted with the cans and cannots of his equipment.

TWIN-LENS REFLEX CAMERAS

The major advantage of the twin-lens reflex is its square, large-size (2¼ X 2¼) format, which removes the problem of horizontal versus vertical, while supplying a good-sized negative or transparency with which to work. These cameras, standbys with many professional photographers, also feature virtual elimination of parallax, a same-size image visible at all times in the picture-taking process, and a very bright image supplied by the viewing lens.

On the debit side of the ledger are bulkiness, noninterchangeability of lenses (on all but one model), and a certain lack of ease of operation. As with other camera types, the twin-lens reflexes can be used for flower photography once their drawbacks are known and compensated for by the photographer.

FOLDING CAMERAS

Expensive folding cameras should be considered for any type of photography, and especially for flower photography. The key to the folding cameras is their cost. Inexpensive folding cameras are nothing more than box cameras that fold to a flat, compact size. The expensive folding cameras offer such things as interchangeable lenses, coupled rangefinders, tilt and swing camera movements to eliminate distortion in flower close-ups, flash and strobe synchronization or both, and large-size film and bellows attachments for in-tight, close-up work. However, like most cameras with separate rangefinders, the possibility of parallax error remains a disadvantage.

Because these sophisticated cameras are true precision instruments, their operation, though physically easy, does require care and practice so they will render good photos. However, this extra care should not be counted as a disadvantage, since all good cameras require care in operation and handling. A definite advantage of this type of camera is its large-format film, usually 620 or 120, large enough for contact printing.

BOX CAMERAS

The simple, easy-to-operate box cameras (which no longer really look like boxes) are good for the very casual snapshooter, but should not be seriously considered for real horticultural photography. Usually requiring no setup time, the box cameras will give clear pictures, but lack all versatility. Since most incorporate only one or two shutter

Mamiya C33 twin lens reflex

speeds and a preset lens opening, it is obvious that these cameras, despite the accessories available, are strictly for the novice and extremely casual snapshooter. However, since there is little or no effort to loading and using these cameras, and since from anywhere back of about 6 feet they give a sharp picture, straight through from this distance to infinity, they should not be considered toys. Instead they can be, and often are, valuable beginner cameras for adults, and teaching cameras for children.

The flexibility of the simple box camera has been increased in some measure by the addition of flash holders (either as a part of the camera itself or attached outside), and through the availability of several different film speeds in both black-and-white and color. Despite these improvements, however, simple box cameras are not suitable for good flower and garden photography, and should therefore be used only for snapshooting.

OTHER CAMERAS

Some of the other cameras available include press and view, single-frame, and ultraminiature. All of these cameras can be used successfully for flower and garden photography, but none are really ideal for this purpose.

The press and view cameras are used mainly by news, studio, portrait, and industrial photographers requiring the utmost in pinpoint sharpness recorded on a large negative. While these cameras provide just about anything a photographer might want—tilts and swings, bellows, interchangeable lenses, and great latitude of both exposure and shutter speed—their price, bulk, and complexity of operation should keep them within the milieu of the professional.

Economy of film and processing costs is the major advantage of the single-frame cameras. This is because they take 72 photos on a regular 36-exposure roll and 40 photos on a 20-exposure roll. They are to be found somewhere between the box camera and the simple rangefinder camera in sophistication and operation. Just about all of the single-frame cameras have completely automatic electric-eye exposure systems (a few have a manual override system) and greatly simplified focusing. They are compact, light, and very easy to carry and operate, but are not ideally suited to flower photography because of the zone focusing. Also, there is the inability to take close-ups (no interchangeable lenses), and the lack of parallax compensation. However, for taking slides for home use and for other casual snapshooting,

Kodak Instamatic box type camera. Flashcube allows four flash shots without changing bulb.

Minox ultra-miniature camera. Bumps on cord indicate distance from lens to subject for close-ups.

it is hard to beat these cameras for economy, simplicity, compactness, and quality of performance.

Even smaller than the small single-frame cameras are the so-called "spy cameras," the ultraminiatures. Producing a negative smaller than a thumbnail, these cameras are precision instruments ideally suited to unobtrusive, candid photography. Included in the features of these cameras are many of the same things expected on a larger, more standard camera—fast lenses, exposure latitude, and flash synchronization. Marvelous because they can be carried with you at all times in a jacket pocket, these cameras make fine second cameras, but should not be counted upon too heavily as primary flower and garden photography equipment.

POLAROID LAND PHOTOGRAPHY

There is not much that can be said about Polaroid Land photography that has not already been said. Polaroids are here to stay! Everyone knows the fabulous Polaroid story—10 seconds after you snap the shutter you hold the finished black-and-whie print in your hand; color takes a bit longer, 60 seconds.

The latest innovation by Polaroid has combined the ultimate in simplicity and sophistication to make poor photos almost obsolete. Some of the many great advantages (some obvious and some not so

19

Polaroid Automatic 100 for color and black and white shots using film pack format.

obvious) include seeing the developed picture almost instantly (if you goof you know it and get a second chance), availability of supplementary lenses that allow close-ups (down to 9 inches), drop-in load film pack, automatic electric-eye exposure (with darken or lighten control), and flash synchronization.

For the best results with the Polaroid cameras it is wise to recognize and learn the proper procedure for pulling the tab and film through the camera. The pull on the tab should be smooth and steady, with no stops, jerks, or interruptions. When this technique is not properly applied, there is a very good chance that blemishes may appear on the developed print and spoil it.

Polacolor prints are finished, complete, and permanent when they come out of the camera 60 seconds after exposure. They require no coating, but for added protection and sturdiness it is a good idea to mount them on the adhesive-coated mounts supplied in each package of film by the Polaroid Corporation.

The addition of the low-priced Swinger to the Polaroid line should place renewed emphasis on black-and-white prints. They need an even, unstreaked plastic coating applied after they are removed from the camera. To assure proper results, this technique also should be learned and mastered. Using the coater packed with each film load, move it across the face of the print in only one direction. Do not stroke it back and forth across the print face. Allow the print to dry thoroughly in a clean, dust-free place before putting one print on top of another.

Remember, Polaroid prints are intended to be used the same size they come from the camera. Therefore, when taking flower and garden photographs, get in close—as close as you possibly can—and don't forget that old trouble-maker parallax! Enlargements in both color and black-and-white are available from the Polaroid Enlargement Service, but except for unusually fine photos, a good close-up, just as it comes from the camera, should be suitable.

If the flower and garden photographer can afford both the conventional camera and a Polaroid, he will have an almost unbeatable team. By using the Polaroid as a "make-sure" camera, the photographer can examine a finished print of his picture in a minute. Although he can see the photo as it will look when finished if he uses an SLR, there is nothing like seeing a finished print to make sure everything is exactly as planned. With the Polaroid print, taken just before an exposure is made with the conventional camera, the flower photographer can make sure of composition, background distractions, lighting, and color, to name just a few.

CAMERA ACCESSORIES

Most cameras are not complete in and of themselves. They are only a part, although a very major part, of what is a complete photographic system. No matter what camera is used, several accessories are important. There are a great many accessories available, many of which are in the "nice-to-have" class. For the purposes of the photographer interested in flower and garden photography, the "must" accessories are: tripod, exposure meter, lens shade, lenses (interchangeable or supplementary), cable release, filters, flash or strobe, and specialized close-up equipment. Since these items will be discussed in later chapters dealing specifically with those areas in which the accessory is a must, short descriptions should suffice at this point.

Tripod—For time exposures, any exposure over 1/50 sec., exposures with large lenses, and most close-ups, a good, steady tripod is considered essential. Prices and styles run the gamut from tiny table-top units to large, bulky professional models. Though pan-tilt heads and other features are a plus item on a tripod, for flower photography look for interchangeable leg tips (pointed metal to dig into earth and rubber for hard surfaces), positive locking legs, and sturdiness.

Exposure Meter—Although there may be a question as to the type of meter to use (incident or reflected), there is no question regarding the indispensability of an exposure meter. Simply put, reflected light meters are pointed away from the camera at the subject (they measure the amount of light reflected from the subject). Incident light meters are held close to the subject and pointed at the camera (they measure the intensity of total light falling on the subject). As a general rule, reflected light meters are better for large outdoor scenes and incident light meters are better for small objects, both indoors and out, when one shoots with available light. Which of the two types you finally choose is up to you, and either one, used correctly, will just about assure better photos.

Lens Shade—Many cameras include a lens shade as standard equipment. If your camera is not one of them, buy one—a lens shade that is, not necessarily another camera. This inexpensive accessory will save many frames of film from being ruined by stray light, especially stray light from sidelighted or backlighted shots or from sunlight reflecting off something and into the camera lens.

Lens—Some method for getting extreme close-ups is a must for successful flower and garden photography. For this reason, lenses of the type compatible with your camera are a good investment. Of the three types, close-up, auxiliary, and interchangeable, interchangeable lenses offer the greatest versatility. Ranging from the super-wide-angle 8mm to a fantastic 1200mm, these interchangeable lenses replace the camera's regular lens (usually about 50mm) and enable the photographer to pick a single perfect bloom from a mass (or mess, as the case may be) of flowers. With the exception of the SLR's, all cameras require special viewfinders for parallax correction and viewing when these "extra" lenses are used.

Auxiliary lenses are used on cameras with permanent lenses, in conjunction with these "normal" lenses. Less expensive than interchangeable lenses, the auxiliary lenses offer some versatility, but require considerable care in viewing and parallax correction.

Close-up lenses, looking very much like clear filters, are also used in conjunction with the permanent camera lenses. These lenses come in various strengths, and can be used either singly or in combination.

When using any of the lenses described here, remember that both parallax correction and pinpoint focusing are critical. Depth of field can become as shallow as a few inches, and parallax correction with a telephoto lens can be considerable; if extreme care is not exercised disaster is probable.

Cable Release—Essential for time exposures and most other shots requiring a camera-on-tripod setup, this inexpensive accessory eliminates camera movement when the shutter is tripped.

Filters—Positioned in front of a lens, a filter stops certain colors from reaching the film while admitting others. It is the accessory that can make the difference between a so-so picture of gray-toned flowers or a prize-winning, sharply contrasted, exciting photo. With over 25 different filters available for black-and-white photography, this accessory will be discussed in depth in the next chapter. Color filters are no less varied. Many filters require exposure compensation, so it is always wise to carefully check the manufacturer's instruction sheet before using or changing filters.

Flash or Strobe—With the exception of occasional mood shots, all indoor flower photography requires some sort of artificial lighting. Indoor lighting will be detailed in a later chapter, so we shall merely indicate here that the availability of flash guns or strobe units, in terms of size, portability, and light output, is limited only by the amount you want to spend.

We have briefly described here the available cameras and the accessories best suited for flower and garden photography. Before buying a new camera, make very certain it will do the job you want it to do, and do it considerably better than the one you own now. Similarly, before buying accessories, determine that they will do the required job, and then double check to see if they are compatible with your camera. Once the camera and accessories are all set, the next item needed to complete the picture is film.

Ektacolor shot of dahlias shows gentle gradation of natural colors.

CHAPTER III

Beauty in Living Color

Although color film is *the* medium for photographing the beauty of nature, getting the best results, the most accurate color rendition, and the most pleasing photos is not quite so simple as some would have you believe. Some photographic principles apply to both color and black-and-white, but many more do not. It is, therefore, better to treat the two kinds of film quite differently.

The very first item on the educational agenda of the photographer planning to use color film is the decision that color must really do something for the photo. Color should not be used for its own sake. Despite the fact that almost all photos can be taken in either black-and-white or color, each type of film has a definite and special place in photography's scheme of things. Black-and-white photography depends for its impact on line, form, and various tones of gray and their contrast. Color photography is less abstract and is designed to record realistically what the eye sees. So if the subject would be more dramatic, more interesting, in black-and-white—use it! Save the color for those occasions when color is *the* thing. Once you decide upon color film, your next decision centers around the different kinds available: their purposes, uses, when and how you want to use them, and what you want to get.

COLOR FILM TYPES

Color film is offered in a wide variety of speeds and types and for use under various specific lighting conditions. Therefore it must become obvious that for the best results the proper selection of color film must be made not only in consideration of the desired end product, but also according to the kind of light under which it is to be exposed.

Reversal films—If your primary interest is in transparencies or slides, the reversal type films are for you. Easily recognizable by the suffix "chrome" in their names (as opposed to the suffix "color" for negative type color film), these films are best processed by either

Giant Fantasy carnation by Crossman Seed.

Unusual view of tulips shot on Kodachrome and printed in black and white.

their own manufacturer or any large, reliable processing company. Some films, such as Anscochrome or Ektachrome, may be processed by the photographer, but this is not recommended for the beginner.

COLOR REVERSAL FILMS

| FILM | TYPE | ASA | AVAILABILITY | |
			35MM	OTHER
AGFACHROME CT 18	FINE GRAIN	50	20X, 30X	120, 620
ANSCOCHROME 50	DAYLIGHT	50	12X, 20X, 36X	120, 127, 620
ANSCOCHROME 100	FAST DAYLIGHT	100	12X, 20X	
ANSCOCHROME T/100	FAST TUNGSTEN	100	12X, 20X	
ANSCOCHROME 200	SUPER FAST TUNGSTEN	200	12X, 20X	
DYNACHROME	FINE GRAIN	25	20X, 36X	
DYNACHROME F	TUNGSTEN	40	20X, 36X	
KODACHROME II	FINE GRAIN	50	20X, 36X	828*
KODACHROME X	FAST DAYLIGHT	64	20X, 36X	*
KODACHROME II F	CLEAR FLASH	10	20X, 36X	*
EKTACHROME X	DAYLIGHT	64	20X, 36X	120, 127, 620, 828
HIGH SPEED EKTACHROME	FAST DAYLIGHT	160	20X, 36X	120
HIGH SPEED EKTACHROME B	TUNGSTEN	125	20X	120
EKTACHROME F	TUNGSTEN	25	20X, 36X	120, 127, 620
TECHNICHROME	FINE GRAIN	25	20X, 36X	

* Also available in cartridges.

The transparencies can be made into prints by exposing them directly onto Kodak Ektachrome paper or Ansco Printon paper. To make a color print from a transparency, an internegative must first be made from the slide, and then prints made in the usual negative manner. While the prints from slides or internegatives are quite good, it is always best to use the film for its primary purpose, with the secondary features utilized only when necessary.

If, however, you do decide to have prints made from transparencies, be sure to select those transparencies that have the best chance of good reproduction. Use original, not duplicate, transparencies when using them for prints, and make certain they are clear, sharp, well exposed, and without heavy shadow areas or overpowering contrasts. Very heavy shadows or dark contrast areas usually show up on the print as black areas. Selecting front-lighted and well-illuminated transparencies will avoid this.

Negative films—The initial end product from these films is a negative, which can be printed in many different ways. The negative films (easily identifiable by the suffix "color") can be exposed by daylight or artificial light and result in extremely realistic color prints. Easier to use and considerably more versatile than reversal film, these films allow color balancing as well as compensation for slight under- or overexposure when the negative is printed.

The versatility of the negative films must be paid for in an additional processing step when anything but prints from the negative is made. Although prints, transparencies, and enlargements can be made from these negatives, the process is relatively expensive. As noted, it is far better to use reversal film for transparencies and negative film for prints and enlargements.

COLOR NEGATIVE FILMS

FILM	ASA	Availability	
		35mm	Other
AGFACOLOR CN 17	40	20X, 36X	120
KODACOLOR X	64	20X	120, 828, 116, 127, 616, 620, cartridge
EKTACOLOR S	80	20X, 36X	120, 620
TECHNICOLOR	32		127, 116, 616
POLACOLOR*	75		Types 48, 38

* Print only, no negative. Duplicates and enlargements made by Polaroid.

COLOR BALANCE

Unlike black-and-white films, which can be exposed under almost all lighting conditions, the available daylight, strobe, and flash-and-flood color films are delicately balanced and may be used only with specific types of lighting. If the film is used under conditions other than those for which it was balanced, the results are usually unsatisfactory with poor color rendition. For example, tungsten film (designed to be used with artificial light) exposed in daylight results in a too-blue photo, and daylight film exposed under artificial light results in a too-yellow picture. This is only one of the problems. The actual color of daylight varies with the angle of the sun, the time of day, and the kind of day (such as clear, cloudy, or hazy). Similarly, there are many different kinds of artificial light, each with different color temperatures than that for which the film was balanced. Although, ideally, every effort should be made to use daylight films outdoors, during the middle of the day, and tungsten film indoors with the correct lights, this is often impossible. It is for just those impossible times that filters step in to balance the light and reestablish the proper proportions for which the film was originally balanced.

REPRESENTATIVE COLOR TEMPERATURES

LIGHT SOURCE		DEGREES KELVIN
CLEAR BLUE SKY		27000
HAZY BLUE SKY		8500
LIGHT OVERCAST SKY		7500
HEAVY OVERCAST SKY		6700
NOON SUNLIGHT		6000
EARLY, LATE SUNLIGHT		5250
ELECTRONIC FLASH		6200*
BLUE FLASHBULB		6000
CLEAR FLASHBULB		3800
WHITE FLUORESCENT		3500
CANDLE		1900
PHOTOFLOOD		3400
TUNGSTEN BULB	500W	2950
TUNGSTEN BULB	100W	2860
TUNGSTEN BULB	60W	2800
TUNGSTEN BULB	40W	2760

* Varies with unit. See data sheet.

FILTERS

Available in a great many colors and sizes, to fit all cameras, filters are divided into several groups. Those of one such group, conversion filters, allow the photographer to use certain films with light sources for which that film was *not* balanced. Color compensating filters change the color balance of the light being used and compensate for any variations in the quality of the light under which the film is exposed. Light balancing filters give the photographer the opportunity to either warm or cool the rendition of the color on the film. All of these filters can be used singly or in combination to arrive at the exact degree of color correction called for by the lighting situation. It should be noted, though, that the use of two or more filters at a single time can cause a distinct loss in definition through light scattering. Always use the least number of filters possible to attain the required color correction.

Skylight filter—The first filter for any flower and garden photographer to buy is the skylight filter. This filter, which requires no exposure increase with any of the daylight color films, should be put in front of the lens and left there whenever color film is shot outdoors. The warming effect of the skylight filter is almost negligible when one shoots in sunlight, but ultraviolet and some of the blue are reduced when one shoots outdoors in shade, giving a more pleasing quality to your photos. Flowers will be recorded in more natural colors, without the bluish tint caused by open shade or the absence of other than skylight illumination. Another feature to consider is the safety factor—it is far cheaper to replace a scratched skylight filter than it is to replace a scratched camera lens that was left unprotected.

Begonia grouping would have been better if color correction filter was used.

CONVERSION FILTER TABLE WITH EXPOSURE INDEXES

FILM	DAY-LIGHT	STROBE	BLUE BULBS	CLEAR BULBS	PHOTO FLOODS	STUDIO LAMPS
KODACHROME II	— 25	— 25	— 25	80C 12	80B 8	80B+82A 12
KODACHROME X	— 64	— 64	— 64	80C 32	80B 20	80B+82A 32
KODACHROME II-A	85 25	NR	NR	81C 30	— 40	82A 32
EKTACOLOR S	— 80	— 80	— 80	80C 40	80B 25	80A 20
EKTACHROME X	— 64	— 64	— 64	80C 32	80B 20	80B+82A 32
HIGH SPEED EKTACHROME	— 160	— 160	— 160	80C 80	NR	NR
HIGH SPEED EKTACHROME B	85B 80	NR	NR	81D 80	81A 100	— 125
EKTACHROME F	85C 16	NR	NR	— 25	82A 16	82C 12
KODACOLOR X*	— 64	85 25	NR	— 50	80B 20	80A 16
ANSCOCHROME D/50	— 50	81A 50	— 50	NR	80B 25	80B+82A 20
ANSCOCHROME D/100	— 100	81A 100	— 100	NR	80B 50	80B+82A 80
ANSCOCHROME T/100	85B 64	NR	85B 64	81D 64	81A 80	— 100
ANSCOCHROME D/200	— 200	81A 200	— 200	NR	80B 100	80B+82A 80
AGFACHROME CT 18	— 50	— 50	— 50	80C 25	80B 25	80B+82A 20
AGFACOLOR CN 17	— 40	85 16	NR	— 40	82A 32	82C 20
POLACOLOR	— 75	— 75	— 75	— 75	80B+12 CC 20B	80B+ 12 CC 20B

Suggested exposure index of film with filter and light combination. Use only as starting point for personal tests.

NR Not recommended.

— None.

* Filters not recommended when developed by Kodak. Use filters on camera when developed at home.

Polarizers—Looking to all the world like neutral gray filters, polarizers can be considered the magicians of photography. For they not only cut down on haze in distant garden shots, they provide the only means for darkening the sky, bringing out cloud effects, and reducing reflections, while pepping up the color saturation of a photo. Usually supplied with a viewer attached to the filter, polarizers allow varying degrees of polarization by rotating the filter 90 degrees. By checking the effect of the filter through the viewer, the photographer can arrive at the correct degree of polarization (it gets greater and greater toward the end of the 90-degree turn). Marvelous backlighted flower shots can be obtained by using a polarizer to eliminate or greatly cut down on the reflections entering the lens. A considerable exposure increase is required with the polarizers, but this is not governed by the amount of filter rotation. A factor of approximately 3X should be used when one shoots color with a polarizer attached to the lens.

While it is true that wonderful things can be done with filters, it is also true that you do not take a once-in-a-lifetime shot using a filter for the first time. The tables accompanying this chapter are designed merely as first steps toward further experimentation by the photographer. In this way, and only in this way, can the photographer accurately learn to predict the results of a filter-light-film combination. And in this way, too, the photographer can arrive at a personal preference, mainly through carefully documented trial-and-error procedures of a film, light source, and filter combination.

COLOR FILTER EXPOSURE INCREASES

COOLING		WARMING	
FILTER	F/STOP INCREASE	FILTER	F/STOP INCREASE
80B	+ 2	81	+ 1/3
80C	+ 1	81A	+ 1/3
82	+ 1/3	81B	+ 1/3
82A	+ 1/3	81C	+ 1/3
82B	+ 2/3	81D	+ 2/3
82C	+ 2/3	85	+ 1-1/2
		85B	+ 2
		85C	+ 1

Film manufacturing differences—Another more or less obvious factor affecting the color rendition of a photo is the brand of film used. Each of the leading manufacturers' films has distinct color characteristics, which must be considered in the light of personal preference and subject matter. Since personal preference is involved, there can be no normal, no right or wrong, but rather a comparison of one brand or type with another, with the eye of the photographer or viewer being the final judge of what is good and what is pleasing color. For example, Agfachrome has pure, clean reds, while Kodachrome II has a more brilliant red, and Dynachrome an almost orange red. Anscochrome 50 is considerably quieter in rendering all colors than its sister Anscochrome 100, whose colors are brighter and cleaner looking.

This type of comparison can be continued for each of the colors of the spectrum and each different color film. The pinpointing of these differences is unnecessary (since they are only important to the photographer's eye), but recognition that these differences exist is necessary. Whatever your final decision, it is entirely up to you, but as with so many other areas of photography, trial and error is the answer. Try many different kinds of film (they differ both in color rendition and color balance) and determine which film you like best and which film best suits the job you want to do.

EXPOSURE

The exposure latitude of color negative films is considerably less than that of black-and-white films. And there is virtually no exposure latitude when one works with reversal type films. As a result, exposure must be almost perfect if you are to get good color rendition—neither underexposed (with resultant heavy, muddy colors) nor overexposed (with washed-out pallid tints). The best recipe for perfect exposure is:

1 set of film manufacturer's instructions
1 exposure meter (either reflected or incident type)
a pinch of knowledge
a heaping portion of care
Mix thoroughly, and add experience.
Gives perfect results every time.

Manufacturer's instructions—Included with each roll of color film is an instruction sheet that includes, among other things, exposure recommendations. These recommendations, along with the other supplementary data, should give well-exposed photos under normal conditions, with average subjects. For many flower and garden color shots,

Reflected light meter used to determine exposure of Ferry Morse tulip bed.

these tables, adjusted a bit to better custom-tailor the lens opening to the conditions at hand, are all that is required for determining the correct lens opening and shutter speed. For all other situations, conditions, and subjects, a reliable exposure meter must be considered a necessity if good color rendition is to be achieved.

Exposure meters—As mentioned in the previous chapter, there are two types of exposure meters—incident light and reflected light meters. The amount of light falling on the subject is measured by an incident light meter held close beside the subject, with the photoelectric cell aimed either at the subject or at the light source. Reflected light meters are aimed at the subject from the position of the camera. It becomes obvious that reflected light meters are accurate for over-all garden shots with the camera some distance away from the subject, while incident light meters are best suited to close-ups of a single flower or two. It should be noted here that reflected light meters are considered to be more accurate for flower and garden photography outdoors than incident light meters, because the incident light meters do not correctly read the light reflected from the various colors of the subject. That is, different colors reflect different amounts of light, and only the reflected light meters are able to get a reliable average reading from this light.

When a reflected light meter is used for flower photos, be certain the background does not overpower the subject and thus affect the

Close-up of Germain's Tickled Pink rose and friend exposed after reading from incident light meter.

meter reading. For example, dark flowers against a light background will be underexposed unless the photographer takes into consideration the effect of the background upon the meter reading, and adjusts for proper subject exposure. Be sure also to consider the sky when you take a meter reading, for it too will have considerable effect on the reading and the resultant exposure. Since a sunless sky is considerably brighter than the flowers or garden being photographed, it is wise to tip the meter down a bit to eliminate the additional brightness. Unless the sky or light background is considered when you take the reading, it is highly probable that the background will be properly exposed while the subject will be badly underexposed.

It is extremely important to realize and remember also that readings taken from either type of exposure meter, as well as the exposure data supplied by the film manufacturer, are not absolute. They are merely starting points to which you can then apply past performance and experience to determine proper lens opening and shutter speed. Consider every part of your subject—the light, dark, and middle tone areas. Check the contrasts between one color and another, between lights and darks, and between shadows and highlights. If an adjustment is required to balance out any extreme, make it and then take your shot. If you are unsure but do not want to take a chance on missing the shot, bracket your photographs. That is, take one shot at the exposure indicated on the meter and two more shots, one a

35

Exposure bracketing gave photographer choice of lighter or darker shot.

full stop more than the reading and the other a full stop less than the reading. In this way, you are pretty sure of getting at least one really good, well-exposed photograph.

Guide numbers—There is considerably less chance for error in the determination of the correct exposure when you use electronic flash or flashbulbs as the light source. Since the light output of these units is practically the same each time, a single number, a guide number, has been specified for each light source–film combination. This guide number, in turn, is used to quickly and easily calculate the correct lens opening.

Each combination of light source (either flashbulb or electronic flash) and film has a specific guide number at a predetermined shutter speed. For example, a certain strobe unit, used with Kodachrome II at 1/60 sec., has a guide number of 40. To find the lens opening (L), divide the guide number (G) by the subject-to-strobe distance (D): $L = \dfrac{G}{D}$. If the strobe is 10 feet from the subject, divide the strobe unit's guide number, 40, by 10. The answer is 4.0, and your f/stop is f/4. Guide numbers are packed with all flashbulbs and strobe units. so finding the correct f/stop is an easy matter.

Fill-in flash—Determining the correct f/stop when you are using fill-in flash outdoors is a bit more complicated than the system described above for flash only, but it is well worth the effort. The fill-in flash technique utilizes the sun as the main light source, and then adds a blue bulb or strobe unit to balance the sun's light so the contrast level of the photo is not too extreme for proper rendition by the film. Flowers can be backlighted or sidelighted by the sun, with light filled in by flash to give a definite feeling of depth and roundness.

To find the correct setup for sunlight plus fill-in flash or strobe, first find the lens opening (L) by taking an exposure meter reading, and set this and the shutter speed on the camera. Since you know the guide number of the flash or strobe (G), the only thing to find is the correct distance of flash to subject (D). The equation then becomes $D = \dfrac{G}{L}$. For the same conditions mentioned previously, the result indicates that the flash or strobe should be placed 10 feet from the subject: $10 \ (D) = \dfrac{40 \ (G)}{4.0 \ (L)}$. This, however, does not mean that the camera need be placed 10 feet from the subject—only the strobe or flash distance has been determined. By use of extension cords, the camera can be placed at almost any desired distance from the subject, just as long as it does not cast a shadow on the subject. If the distance between the subject and the flash is too great as a result of the brightness of the flash, it can be reduced by placing a clean white handkerchief over the reflector. A single layer of handkerchief will reduce the amount of light by the equivalent of one f/stop, two layers by about two f/stops. *Do NOT* change the f/stop you set after taking the meter reading. The equivalents mentioned here are only for computing the distance of flash to subject. The f/stop is the same as before, as it came from the meter reading. This change in f/stop equivalent means that the distance of the flash or strobe can be shortened, bringing it closer to the subject. Using the same example:

(1) Without handkerchief, 10 feet (D) $= \dfrac{40 \ (G)}{4.0 \ (L)^*}$

(2) With one layer of handkerchief, 7 feet (approx.) $D = \dfrac{40 \ (G)}{5.6 \ (L)^{**}}$

(3) With two layers of handkerchief, 5 feet (D) $= \dfrac{40 \ (G)}{8 \ (L)^{**}}$

* Actual f/stops for all three examples.

** Equivalent f/stops—used only to compute flash-to-subject distance.

Multiple flash instead of single flash on camera should have been used for desert shot.

Single handkerchief used to cut down light from strobe on cymbidium orchids.

CARE AND HANDLING

Environmental factors have a considerable effect on film, especially color film. Heat and moisture are the prime offenders, but certain gases, X-rays, and other factors can also cause film deterioration. Because color film is manufactured with three distinct emulsion layers, exposure of the film to heat or moisture can cause changes in color balance, in film speed, and in contrast. It then becomes obvious why it is so important to correctly store, handle, and care for photographic film before use, after use, and after processing.

Before use—The original packages in which color film is sold will protect the film against humidity—if the film cans or sealed tin-foil bags are left unopened. There is no reason to open the film carton or the inner protector before you are ready to use the film.

Heat poses a different problem from that caused by moisture. Original packages and cans offer little or no protection against high heat. Color film should not, therefore, be stored for more than 4 weeks in an area where the temperature is over 70°. Keep film in a cool, dry place, away from steam pipes, stoves, or other high-heat sources. When on a trip, keep film out of closed cars and especially out of the glove compartment. The extreme heat that can build up in these closed areas will, after just a few hours, cause considerable damage to the color balance and speed of the film.

When film is to be stored for a considerable time prior to use, or the temperature in your region will be high for a long period, store unopened packages of film in the refrigerator, or for even longer periods, in the freezer. Whether the refrigerator or freezer is used, remember to allow the film to stand after removal until it reaches room or air temperature. The package should then be opened and the film therein used as quickly as possible. Do not remove the film package from the refrigerator or freezer or open the package until just before you are ready to use it. To help in gauging the time required to bring the film to room temperature, allow approximately 1 hour for a temperature rise of 25°, and approximately 1½ hours for a rise of 100°. When you bring the film up to room temperature, stand it on end so air can circulate freely around the package. Do not stack packages one on top of the other, as this limits air circulation and additional time will be required to thaw out the film.

If the film has not been used but the can has been opened or the film taken out of the container, it can be affected by many chemicals, including motor exhausts, solvents, cleaners, and mildew or fungus preventatives. If the film must be kept in areas where it might be

U.S. *Forest Service.* Leaves and fruit of Alleghany chinkapin.

exposed to these harmful gases, placing the film in tightly closed jars will give adequate protection.

The suggestion of the film manufacturers that film be used before the expiration date printed on the carton should be taken not as a suggestion but as a command. While there is the chance that the film may still be good after the expiration date, the chances are also good that the film speed will be off, as might be the color balance and rendition capability. Simply stated, it is a lot cheaper and wiser to throw out expired film than it is to use it and find, too late, that the film was indeed no good.

After use—Film should be removed from the camera and processed as soon as possible after exposure. Since the film is no longer protected by the film can or the package, it is open to attack by all the aforementioned environmental conditions. Film is also affected by sudden changes in temperature, so when you leave an air-conditioned building and enter the heat of the day, allow sufficient time for any condensation to be evaporated. Check your lens, too, it may also be coated with a fine mist of condensation.

A bit of common sense will stand the photographer in good stead when he sends film for processing. Since exposed film is even more susceptible to damage from heat and moisture than is the unexposed film, see that it gets to the processor as quickly as possible. If the film is to be mailed, check the pickup time on the mailbox. Try to deposit the film in the box as near to pickup time as possible so it does not remain in the closed, hot mailbox for a long period. Dropping it off directly at the post office is the best idea, if this is possible. Once out of the mailbox, air mail will speed the film quickly to its destination, so use this method, especially during hot and humid weather.

After processing—Processed color films are also affected by their environment, especially by heat, light, and moisture. It therefore makes good sense to store processed color film in a cool, dry, dark place. This rules out most cellars (which are damp) and attics (which allow heat to build up). Also ruled out are areas that contain moth balls or other forms of paradichlorobenzene, insecticides, and fungicides. The chemicals contained in these preparations can cause irreparable damage to slides and negatives.

Do not handle color slides or negatives excessively. When handling is necessary, touch the edges only. Transparencies that have been mounted should be put into the projector magazine and kept free of dirt and dust. Negatives should be kept in protective plastic or glassine sleeves, with the sleeves marked for easy negative identification.

To protect color slides, avoid projecting a single slide for times in excess of one minute. Little damage will be done if slides are projected many, many times, but overlong projection of a slide subjects it to extreme light and heat, which can ruin the slide or at the very least make colors fade and distort the transparency.

If properly handled, stored, and cared for, color photographic materials will remain stable almost indefinitely, but without this attention their life span is considerably shortened.

Antherium shot on Ektacolor printed on Kodak Polycontrast Rapid.

CHAPTER IV

Opportunities in Black-and-White

After a discussion of photographing flowers and gardens in color, noting the various ways to get good or better photos, a similar discussion of black-and-white photography might seem superfluous. In truth, it is not. Color and black-and-white films should be considered not as brothers but as distant cousins. There are a great many pluses and minuses that can be attached to either medium. Although they are allied in many ways, they are also different in many ways, and that is the key. They are different and should be treated as such.

How is it possible for some photographers to say that almost any picture can be taken in either black-and-white or color? The answer can be found in another question: What do you want to show in your finished picture? If you want an extremely realistic rendition, closely akin to what the eye sees, then you want color. If you want something dramatic or graphic without too much consideration of actual colors, your best bet is black-and-white.

BLACK-AND-WHITE FILMS

Once decided on black-and-white film, the photographer has a fantastic range of films from which to choose. He can select, according to the camera and the job to be done, from slow, fast, or medium speeds; fine, coarse, or medium grain; panchromatic or orthochromatic types (infrared and process are available but are only used for special purposes); and, of course, sheet, roll, cartridge, or film pack loads.

Panchromatic and Orthochromatic Films—Perhaps the most difficult part of flower photography in black-and-white is the realization that the results will not be in color or even in true tones of black-and-white, but rather in varying tones of gray. And even this miracle of rendering full color in tones of gray is not complete, since there is at least one small shortcoming remaining in all available films.

Malak. The mood of this tulip photo is enhanced by black and white rendition. Color would hinder, not help here.

The so-called "pan" or panchromatic films are the most widely used of the black-and-white films. The reason is that these are the only films sensitive to practically all colors. The shortcomings here affect the rendition of red, blue, and green (red and blue come out a bit lighter and green a bit darker than they should), but these can be easily corrected through the use of filters.

Orthochromatic films are used considerably less often than panchromatic because of their insensitivity to red (it renders it black) and blue (it comes out almost white). While some of this insensitivity can be corrected by filters, the over-all quality of these films is lower than that of the panchromatic films, making them inferior to the more widely used pan films.

Film Speed—Currently on the market are black-and-white films that run the speed gamut from less than 10 to 1250, and Polaroid's 3000. For the flower and garden photographer, indeed for all photographers, the choice of film should be made on the basis of the job

44

Very difficult to shoot in color, this Lord and Burnham greenhouse is effective in black and white.

to be done and the conditions under which it will be done. Because of the gradual increase in graininess as the speed goes up, and the gradual softening of gradation as well, the photographer should always choose the slowest film he can to do the job at hand. By selecting the slowest film possible, the photographer gives himself a better chance of making excellent prints and enlargements from even the smallest negatives. Of course, as the negative size increases from 35mm to 2¼ X 2¼ and up, the acuteness of the grain problem decreases rapidly.

The very slow films, such as Agfa Isopan FF (ASA 25) and Adox KB-14 (ASA 20), make very fine negatives and result in virtually grain-free enlargements, even at extreme sizes. Unfortunately, with films this slow the shutter speed must be dropped and the diaphragm opened up. With this kind of a setup, the slightest breeze or movement of a flower will usually cause a blurry photo.

The next group, or slow films, include, among others, Kodak Panatomic-X (ASA 40), Ilford Pan F (ASA 50), and Adox KB-17 (ASA 40). While not losing much in graininess or sharpness (resolution), these films allow hand holding of cameras more readily, and are generally excellent to use in good lighting situations; they are especially good for use with high-guide-number electronic flash units.

The most widely used, and perhaps the best all-around films, fall into the medium-speed grouping. Agfa Isopan SS (ASA 200), Kodak Plus-X (ASA 125), and Adox KB-21 (ASA 100) are representative films in this class. As we noted in the general discussion of films, graininess goes up with film speed, and while the increased grain in big enlargements from this film is far from obvious, it is still there to a greater degree than with the slower films. These medium-speed films mark the entrance of available light photography, and "pushing" of film (changing the ASA number upward, and developing accordingly).

The high-speed films, such as Kodak Tri-X (ASA 400) and Ansco Super Hypan (ASA 500), are fast enough for available light photography, and still slow enough to be used under certain almost-normal lighting conditions with many cameras. Though a good 8 X 10 enlargement can be made of this film from a 35mm negative, grain is obvious to the eye. Unless the photographer actually wants the grain effect, or is shooting flowers under very poor lighting conditions (which is not often), he should stick to the films in the medium and slower speed classes.

If, for some reason, you want soft, grainy photos, the very-high-speed films, such as Ilford HPS (ASA 800) and Agfa Isopan Record (ASA 1250), will give this kind of result with little extra work on your part. It is difficult to conceive of a situation in which either flowers or gardens would be photographed requiring this kind of extreme film speed and resulting questionable end product. If, however, such situations should arise, these films are available for those who want them.

As the table of black-and-white films shows, there are films available for every use and every lighting situation. It is here that the wise photographer makes a careful decision—he selects the slowest speed film he can under the lighting conditions at hand. At the same time, he takes into consideration the shutter speed he would like to use and whether or not he is going to use filters. By this careful selection, he places himself in a good position to get good photos and then satisfactory enlargements.

46

High speed film and cleverly placed Westinghouse bulbs in watertight sockets
produce dramatic results.

47

BLACK-AND-WHITE FILMS

FILM	TYPE	ASA D/T	AVAILABILITY 35MM	OTHER
ADOX KB-14*	VERY SLOW, ULTRA FINE GRAIN	20/16	20X, 36X	
KB-17	SLOW, FINE GRAIN	40/32	20X, 36X	
KB-21	MEDIUM, GOOD CONTRAST	100/80	20X, 36X	
AGFA ISOPAN FF	VERY SLOW, FINE GRAIN	32/24	20X, 36X	120
ISOPAN F	MEDIUM, WIDE LATITUDE	100/80	20X, 36X	120, 127, 620
ISOPAN SS	MEDIUM, GOOD CONTRAST	200/160	36X	120, 127, 620
ISOPAN ULTRA	FAST, HIGH RED SENSITIVITY	400/800	36X	120, 127
ISOPAN RECORD	ULTRA HIGH SPEED	1250/	36X	120
ANSCO ALLWEATHER PAN	MEDIUM, GENERAL USE	125/100		120, 127, 620, 616
VERSAPAN	MEDIUM, GOOD RENDITION	125/125	20X	
SUPER HYPAN	FAST, GOOD GRAIN	500/400	20X, 36X	120, 620
GEVAERT GEVAPAN 27	SLOW, FINE GRAIN	40/32		120
GEVAPAN 30	MEDIUM, FINE GRAIN	125/100		120, 127, 620
GEVAPAN 33	MEDIUM, LONG GRADATION SCALE	250/160		120, 127, 620
GEVAPAN 36	FAST, GOOD GRAIN	400/320		120, 127, 620
X-L PAN	MEDIUM, ALL PURPOSE	125/100		120, 127, 620
ILFORD PAN F	SLOW, VERY FINE GRAIN	50/	20X, 36X	127
FP 3	MEDIUM, FINE GRAIN	125/	20X, 36X	127
HP 3	FAST, FINE GRAIN	400/	20X, 36X	127
HPS	VERY FAST, GOOD GRADATION	800/	36X	

Tulips of the "Dutch Princess" or "Triumph" variety.   PHOTO BY MALAK, OTTAWA

Landscape-gardening contest winner.

Lilium-Georgia Belle, taken with electric flash and 1 lens polarizer; 1/125 sec. at f/16.

Two varieties of home-grown roses—the Elinor LeGrice and the Pink Duchess Tree Rose.

Chunking Narcissi (Small Cup), taken with electric flash and 1 lens polarizer; 1/125 sec. at f/16.

Cluster of Croci—the Yellow Crocus, the white Joan of Arc, and the blue Remembrance.

FILM	TYPE	ASA D/T	AVAILABILITY	
			35MM	OTHER
KODAK PANATOMIC X	SLOW, FINE GRAIN	40/32	20X, 36X	120, 127, 620, 828
PLUS X	MEDIUM, FINE GRAIN	125/80	20X, 36X	
VERICHROME PAN	MEDIUM, GENERAL USE	125/100		120, 127, 620, 828
TRI-X	FAST, GOOD GRAIN	400/320	20X, 36X	120, 127, 620, 828
ROYAL-X PAN	VERY FAST	1250/		120, 620
SUPREME VARIPAN 25	VERY SLOW, FINE GRAIN			
VARIPAN 50	SLOW, FINE GRAIN			
VARIPAN 100	MEDIUM, GENERAL USE			
VARIPAN 250	MEDIUM, GOOD GRAIN			
POLAROID LAND TYPE 37	FOR J33, 80, 80A, 80B, CAMERAS, 10-SEC. DEVEL	3000		
TYPE 47	FOR ALL OTHER CAMERAS	3000		
POLAPAN TYPE 32	FOR 80, 80A, 80B	400		
POLAPAN TYPE 42	ALL BUT J33, J66	200		
POLAPAN TYPE 44	ALL BUT J33, J66, 80, 80A, 80B	400		
TYPE 107	FOR FILM PACK CAMERAS	3000		

* Adox R-14, 17, 21, same speed as KB series but available in 120.

COLOR RENDITION

Despite the fact that the panchromatic films are sensitive to almost all colors, they do require some help in rendering certain colors lighter or darker than other colors. As is the case with color film, filters are available for black-and-white film. Simply stated, filters pass light of their own color and absorb light of other colors. With this in mind, it becomes reasonably easy for the photographer to select the correct filter for the effect he is trying to achieve. Thus if he wants to make the color lighter he uses a filter of the same color, and if he wants to make it darker he uses a filter of a different color, preferably a darker one.

Magnificent whiteness of Jackson and Perkins' John F. Kennedy rose is accentuated through the use of a yellow filter.

Filters—Two distinct groups of filters are available for use with black-and-white films—contrast filters and correction filters.

Contrast filters are used to make specific colors lighter or darker, to either exaggerate a color rendition or subdue it, thus enhancing another color. This type of filter is of special interest to flower and garden photographers. When you shoot a white flower against a blue sky, there will be little definition, shape, or form, since pan films render both the white and the light blue almost the same very light gray. A yellow filter will darken the sky, bringing out the whiteness of the flower. Similarly, red flowers against a green foliage background come out unsatisfactory on black-and-white film. If you use a green filter, the green leaves will be lighter and the red flowers will stand out.

50

FILTERS FOR USE WITH BLACK-AND-WHITE FILMS

FILTER	WRAT-TEN NUM-BER	USE	FILTER FACTOR AVERAGE		FILM	
			SUN	TUNG.	ORTHO.	PAN.
LT YELLOW	K1	DARKEN SKY, BRING OUT CLOUDS	1.5	1.5	X	X
MED YELLOW	K2	HEIGHTEN CONTRAST OF SKY AND FOLIAGE	2.5	2	X	X
YELLOW	K3	DRAMATIC SKY	2.5	2	X	X
DEEP YELLOW	G	VERY DRAMATIC SKY	5	3	X	X
LT GREEN	X1	NATURAL FLOWERS, BLOSSOMS	4	3		X
GREEN	X2	LIGHTEN FOLIAGE	5	4		X
DK GREEN	B	VERY LIGHT FOLIAGE	8	5		X
RED	A	DETAIL RED, ORANGE BLOOMS	8	4		X
DARK RED	F	DETAIL OF FLOWER, SUBDUE FOLIAGE	16	8		X
BLUE	C5	ADD HAZE, BRING OUT DETAILS	5	10	X	X

* Check with film information sheet for filter factors of specific films.

SUBJECT COLOR	FILTER TO MAKE LIGHTER	FILTER TO MAKE DARKER
RED	F, A, G	B, C5
GREEN	G, B, X1, X2	A, C5
BLUE	C5	B, A, G, F
GREEN-BLUE	C5, B	A, F
DEEP PINK	A, F	B
VIOLET	C5	B
YELLOW	A, G	C5
ORANGE	A, G	C5

Correction filters are not usually used to exaggerate colors, but rather to normalize them. The correction filters are designed to render colors in the tone of gray equivalent to the way the color actually looks to the eye. Red and blue appear darker to the eye than does green, but on film the green appears darker than the red or blue. To remedy this situation, the photographer would use a green filter to lighten the green and darken the red and blue.

Both contrast and correction filters should be used singly and not in combination with any but polarizing filters. If used in combination with other color filters, not enough light will get through to expose the film properly.

In addition to the filters already mentioned for use with black-and-white films, are polarizers and haze and neutral density filters. The polarizers and haze filters are the same as those used for color photography. Neutral density filters are used to cut down the amount of light of all colors reaching the film, when the film is of too high a speed to allow proper exposure under high light conditions. For example, if you use a camera with a lens whose smallest f/stop is f/20 and Tri-X film in bright sunlight, the combination would result in an f/stop smaller than f/20, say f/32. By use of a neutral density filter, the color is unchanged, less light is allowed through, and the proper exposure can be made.

Since flower and garden photography in black-and-white depends a great deal on proper color rendition, the use of filters becomes almost mandatory if pleasing results are to be achieved. The great variety of flower colors prohibits actual listing of filter-film combinations. However, once the photographer learns how each color will appear in black-and-white, he can make his selection of filters according to the results desired. In this way, he can lighten or darken the leaves or the blooms, lighten or darken the background, or do the many other things that will make his subject stand out and show the marvelous detail inherent in nature.

EXPOSING AND DEVELOPING

Much of what has been said concerning exposure for color applies to black-and-white; repetition is unnecessary. Suffice it to say that careful use of the exposure meter and intelligent development by the photographer or reliable laboratory should result in fine photos. In this vein, it is wise to spend a bit more for custom development than to risk a roll of film on run-of-the-mill drugstore development.

Parella's Dr. P. P. Pirone dahlia would be less than its beautiful self without proper color correction for reproduction in black and white.

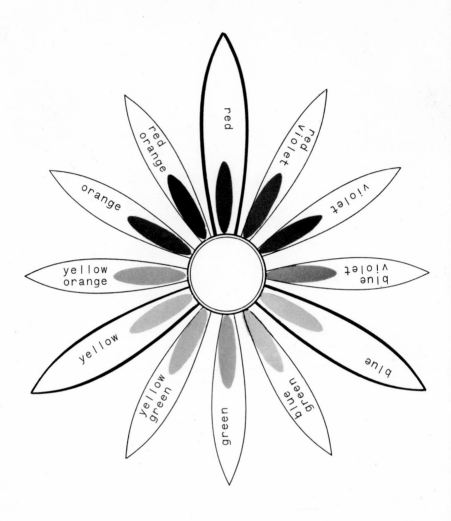

This color wheel flower shows how Panchromatic film translates the colors most often found in flowers into tones of black and white.

Taken at Sterling Forest Gardens, this shot is passable in color, awful in black and white.

If the pictures were worth taking, they are worth developing correctly. You can help yourself by helping the processing lab. Include a note with your film indicating the ASA number at which you shot and the lighting conditions under which the film was exposed. The lab can then develop the film according to this information, giving you better negatives and more beautiful prints.

COMPOSITION

Though much of the information given in the chapter on composition applies to both color and black-and-white, special emphasis should be placed on black-and-white composition. While an occasional poorly composed color shot can be saved by the colors, this is impossible with black-and-white. Remember that your photo must be balanced and pleasing to view, and must have enough contrast to make it interesting if not dramatic. See that highlights are clean, and dark areas dense. Check to see that the background adds to the over-all effect and does not detract or confuse the photo. Remember that, especially in black-and-white, one close-up is worth 10,000 globs of gray. And, above all, when you shoot flowers and gardens, use your imagination and creativity to show the beauty of nature in a manner that really does it justice.

National Orchid Growers Association float, an orchid Ferris Wheel at Miss America Pageant.

CHAPTER V

Composition and Nature

There is often little that a photographer can do about rearranging one of nature's settings. He can do much, however, to get the most pleasing photo from the elements at hand. It is in this area, the area of photographic composition, that the photographer gets his greatest chance at self-expression and creativity. The snapshooter will be content with gobs and gobs of colorful flowers all over his photos. But the snapshooter is also quite pleased when his pictures come out.

The photographer wants something better. He is not content to leave the composition of his flower and garden photos to luck, or to the whim and fancy of nature. Similarly, the photographer refuses to have his hands tied by a set of hard-and-fast rules governing photographic composition. Instead, there are several points that serve as a guide, and these, coupled with the photographer's eye, should result in pictures that are interesting and pleasing to the viewer.

COMPOSITION HINTS AND TIPS

One guide that cannot be stressed enough is the importance of simplicity when one is composing flower and garden photographs. Simplicity should be the byword in composition and arrangement—and, as a matter of fact, in all photography. It is far better to show one or two beautiful blooms than it is to cram every part of a plant or an entire garden into a single picture. For what is proven when everything is jammed into a photo? Very little, since when the picture is projected, the viewer will see a great many distracting small elements making up a large distracting picture.

Main feature—Simplicity also enters into the determination of the dominating feature or main point of interest of each photo. There should be only one dominating feature in each photo, and it should be prominent, with all other elements clearly subordinate. It is wise to include some secondary interest, but this must be in balance and harmony with the primary point of interest, never detracting from the over-all effect.

Two views of the same garden show the difference a viewpoint can make.

FERRY-MORSE SEED CO.

59

Nature itself gives adequate clues to a good arrangement of many flowers. Very often the way a flower grows, and its structure, constitute the best possible arrangement. Since the flower is the culmination of the life cycle of a plant, some of the other parts of the cycle would make for a more complete, more interesting photo.

In this kind of photo, for example, the fully opened flower is in the position of dominance, with foliage, tightly closed buds, and partially opened buds in subordinate but complementary positions. Everything must lead the eye toward the dominating bloom, or else, instead of a picture story complete in one photo, the result will be a hodgepodge of disconnected elements.

Camera Placement—Another facet of composition, one in which the photographer has considerable freedom, is the placement of the camera. On occasion, as when the photographer is shooting wild flowers or in certain highly cultivated gardens, there is little room to move. However, in all other cases the photographer should carefully check out various positions, angles, and views. A considerable difference in the composition of a photograph can be seen when the position of the camera is changed, and this must be taken into account when one is composing. For example, a beautiful rose shot head-on would appear as the dominant element in a photo of a rose bush. However, shot from another angle, such as the side, the dominant feature changes completely, presenting an entirely different photo.

Garden photography is particularly susceptible to composition changes resulting from perspective distortions. Since the borders, hedges, or groupings will, because of size, have to be in the background, the foreground will appear proportionately large. To the eye, this composition may be quite satisfactory. However, the camera will record it as a large expanse of foreground with a relatively small background. As a result, your subject will appear subordinate to the foreground. By repositioning the camera on a different angle to the subject, the balance and perspective will be corrected and the photo will be considerably better.

Distracting elements—Another item to be checked in the viewfinder, when you are composing a picture, is the presence of unsightly gaps or holes. Unless the photographer deliberately looks for this sort of thing, his eye will not see it. However, the camera's eye will, and on the finished photo they will be real eyesores. Some imagination will help remedy this situation, if it cannot be eliminated entirely by changing the camera angle. A bit of foliage from another part of the plant or a few flowers can be wired into place by the photographer

M. C. Feinstein. Fuller's Teasel both in and out of focus makes interesting photo.

to cover the open areas. If this is done, be sure the wiring handiwork is carefully carried out, and either out of the picture or completely concealed.

As previously mentioned, for good composition and a pleasing photo everything must be in harmony. That is, the dominant feature, the supporting elements, and the background must all be combined to create a complete photo. Competition among any or all of these elements will break apart the composition and detract from the photo.

Balance and harmony—When you set up your subject, never place it in the exact center of the picture. A much better place is a bit off-center, where it will be more interesting and command more

Extraneous light areas detract from these peony blossoms.

R. J. BODEN

attention. Similarly, the total picture should be uneven, but balanced, in its area distribution. The areas of each color, whether you use black-and-white or color film, should balance each other on either side of the imaginary axis, but the breakup of each area should be uneven. The same is true of the subject when you shoot flowers. For example, three small red flowers at the top photo left can be very satisfactorily balanced by a single large red flower at bottom photo right. Just as you should balance a color photo with warm and cool colors, you should balance a black-and-white photo by using the various light and dark areas. Neither all the light nor all the dark areas should fall in a single portion of the photo. Considerable interest will be added to the photo if the lights and darks are broken up and balance the entire composition.

While we are on the subject of light and dark areas, a few more compositional hints should be noted. Although they may be exactly the same size, light spots on a dark background attract more attention than dark spots on a light background. Remember this when you shoot light or white flowers and choose an appropriate background.

Similarly, shadows and light patterns should be used where they will do the most good. Used correctly, shadows can point up those areas of central interest, or give an almost third-dimensional effect to flower portraits. Conversely, if used incorrectly, shadows and light patterns can be extremely disconcerting and, in some cases, attract more attention than the subject. If you intend to use the shadows for a special effect and require a specific kind of shadow or light effect, it would be wise to schedule your shooting sessions outdoors for certain times of day. During midday, the shadows are sharper, denser, and better defined. Early in the morning and late in the afternoon, the sun is at an angle and the shadows are softer and longer. By anticipating where and how shadows will fall, you can actually use them in your flower photos as integral parts of the subject and of the composition.

Leading the eye—Lines, where they go and what they do, are also to be considered when you compose a flower or garden photo. Light and shadow have direction and should lead the eye to the photo's dominant features; lines should be used for the same purpose. The eye will follow the direction of a line, whether it is the form of a branch, a light pattern, or the shingles on a house. For this reason, if possible, it is preferred that the viewer's eye be led into the photo and eventually to the subject from the lower left-hand side of the photo. For

U.S. Forest Service. Paper birches along roadway.

reasons too involved to detail here, entrance at this point is natural, and will make the photo seem more natural.

Other interesting lines can be used to attract the eye and then lead it either to the subject or to another special feature of the photo. But, here too, the eye should be led without the device being too obvious. Avoid lines that run in the opposite direction from the subject and lines that run out of the picture, unless they lead into the subject and continue on through. If two lines are used, such as those forming a road, do not let them run parallel to the bottom edge of the picture. Instead of showing the parallel lines, which are distracting and create dual interest points, shoot the road from an angle at the end of which is the subject. A large tree at the end of a road can make a beautiful photo if the lines of the road seem to converge and lead the eye to the subject.

Good positioning helps make good close-up on Harris cactus dahlia.

An important line to watch is the horizon line. It should not be allowed to divide a photo in half, since this would result in two equal halves and a considerably less interesting photo. More interest will be generated if the horizon line comes either one-third of the way down from the top or one-third of the way up from the bottom.

Helping nature—Very often there appear to be hundreds of beautiful photos in a garden, but when you get close or examine them in the viewfinder they are just not what you want. In cases like this, it is entirely cricket to give nature a helping hand. If the flowers are spread too far apart to give the massed color effect you want on color film, some of the plants may be transplanted, or additional plants may be added to the area.

Flowers that are not arranged suitably or are in the wrong position can be adjusted to make a better photo. A few thin sticks or dowels

Two views of the same rose garden at Sterling Forest shows the differences made by camera placement.

can be used to prop the flowers into a more desirable position. Twist-ems can be used to secure the stalks to the sticks while you shoot, and then can be removed to allow the plants to return their normal positions.

Be sure that the area at the base of a plant or bush is well groomed. A beautiful photo of a bush is easily ruined by light, sandy-looking, or rocky soil at the base. Before shooting, cover the area with peat moss and wet down thoroughly, and you will have a beautiful, dark, photogenic base for your photos.

These are just some of the things that can be done by the photographer who is trying to create beautiful flower and garden photos by improving their composition. Although they are mentioned briefly in other chapters, backgrounds will now be discussed in some detail because of their importance in the composition and total effect of a photo.

GOTTSCHO-SCHLEISNER, INC.

BACKGROUNDS

Nothing will spoil a good flower and garden photo faster than a poor background. For this reason, backgrounds should be carefully considered and selected on the basis of their impact on each different picture.

The number and kinds of backgrounds available are virtually unlimited. In the out-of-doors the sky, an expanse of lawn, foliage, and many other things can be used as background for either single flowers or entire gardens. Whatever is selected, it should be simple, easily blended, and a complement to any part of the total picture. Where the background is going to be out of focus, make sure it does not contain large areas of light or dark that can distract from the subject. Be sure also that some background detail is not in a position to make the photo ludicrous. That is, a pole or tree should not be allowed to appear as if it is growing out of some person's head.

Probably the best backgrounds for individual flowers or plants are large colored cardboards for color photos and gray cardboards for black-and-white. Put far enough away from the subject, they will be out of focus and can simulate sky, earth, or foliage.

Indoors, similar cardboards can be used for table-top photography of flowers, with the foreground being faked through the use of peat moss, stones, and dirt. When you work with these cardboards, especially indoors, be certain that either they are far enough away from the

FERRY-MORSE SEED CO.

All American Thumbelina zinnias seem to belong in this simple setting.

subject so no distracting shadows fall, or special lights are aimed at the background to wash out shadow areas.

Whatever the background chosen, either real or artificial, it should look real—it should never appear fake or faked. If a cloth background is used, be sure there are no wrinkles and no deep creases caused by careless hanging. Similarly, if cardboard is used, make certain whatever paper pattern is on the surface is softened sufficiently by its being out of focus to assure that there is no distraction.

CROPPING

One of the standard darkroom procedures can be used very effectively as a composition tool. Cropping gives the photographer the opportunity of selecting the portion of the negative that best suits him while discarding the remainder. By cropping the final print, you can recompose an over-all record shot into one of pictorial importance, or you can merely select the most important portion of the photo, eliminating unnecessary areas, distractions, or details. This kind of cropping will give good, dramatic results from any so-so originals. By experimenting with the negative projected onto a printing easel, or by using a contact sheet made from an entire roll of film, you can pick and choose exactly the area you want in your finished photo.

U.S. Forest Service. Flowers of American chestnut tree.

CHAPTER VI

Getting in Close

Few objects exemplify beauty and order better than a close-up of a single perfect bloom. The ability to shoot this kind of photograph can open up a whole new world of dramatic beauty—the beauty of design, pattern, texture, color, and individuality. This world, however, is not available without effort, mixed well with care. This does not mean merely the normal care exercised in photography; it means an extremely meticulous brand of care, for when you shoot close-ups the slightest error can result in failure. One part of the care required for successful close-up photography is the selection of the correct equipment to do the job; other parts include the techniques of photography—viewing, focusing, and exposing.

Close-up photography can be divided into three distinct categories—close-ups (the subject is reproduced from a reduced size to same size), macrophotography (from same size to about 25 times actual size), and microphotography (anything over 25 times actual size). Since flowers are best reproduced at approximately same size, our purposes are best served by discussing only that portion of photography dealing with close-ups, and allowing the other areas full discussion in other, specialized books dedicated to those specialties.

EQUIPMENT

Almost any camera can be used to take close-ups of flowers. Even Brownies, when helped along, can be used. Naturally, the more expensive, more versatile adjustable cameras will do a better job, and will do it with greater speed, convenience, and reliability. For all simple cameras, and for many adjustable cameras as well, you will need supplementary lenses and a means of determining exact focus, distance, and view.

Lenses—Close-up supplementary lenses look like clear filters and are almost as easy to use. Available in various strengths, these lenses are attached directly in front of the camera lens either singly or in combination. Using the table that follows, which is designed for use with Kodak Portra lenses, you can see that a 1+ lens allows you to get as close as 40 inches, 2+ as close as 20 inches, and 3+ as close

71

as 13 inches. By combining, for example, a 2+ and a 3+ Portra lens, you can get as close as 8 inches from the subject, with a field size of 3⅞ X 5¾. Notice also, however, that the depth of field is extremely shallow, only ½ in. from 7¾ to 8¼ inches, so focusing must be exact. For lenses other than the Kodak Portra, use the tables provided with the close-up lenses. When you use close-up lenses in combination, always put the stronger lens closest to the camera. In the above example, the 3+ goes on first, next to the camera, and then the 2+.

Lily of the valley, extremely close-up.

John F. Kennedy rose by Jackson & Perkins.

SUPPLEMENTARY LENS DATA FOR 35mm CAMERAS
AND KODAK PORTRA LENSES

LENS OR LENSES	CAMERA FOCUS	SUBJECT-TO-LENS DISTANCE (INCHES)	DEPTH OF FIELD (INCHES)	APPROXIMATE FIELD SIZE (INCHES)
+3	INF	13	12½ — 14	6¼ X 9¼
	FIXED*	12¼	11½ — 12¾	5¾ X 8¾
	4	10⅜	10 — 11	5 X 7½
+2	INF	19½	18½ — 22	9½ X 14
	FIXED*	17¾	16½ — 20	9½ X 14
	4	14	13 — 15	8½ X 13
+1	INF	39	35 — 48	19 X 28
	FIXED*	32½	28 — 38	13 X 19
	4	21½	20 — 25	9½ X 14
+3 + 1	INF	10	9⅝ — 10⅜	4¾ X 7
	FIXED*	9	8¾ — 9⅜	4½ X 6½
	4	8¼	8 — 8½	4 X 6
+3 + 2	INF	8	7¾ — 8¼	3⅞ X 5¾
	FIXED*	7¾	7½ — 8	3¾ X 5½
	4	7	6¾ — 7¼	3⅜ X 5⅛
+3 + 3	INF	6½	6¼ — 6⅝	3⅛ X 4¾
	FIXED*	6¼	6⅛ — 6⅜	3 X 4½
	4	5¾	5½ — 5⅝	2⅞ X 4¼

* Fixed focus (15 feet) for simple cameras.

Extension Tubes—Available in a variety of sizes and materials, these tubes can only be used on cameras with interchangeable lenses, since one end fits the camera's lens mount and the other the lens. Inexpensive, these tubes can be used singly or in combination, but only on certain types of cameras. They cannot be used on twin-lens reflexes, cameras with between-the-lens shutters, and Contaflex type SLR's. Since the extension tubes are rigid they are quite sturdy, but

74

the focusing movement is limited to the small amount of movement available on the lens itself.

Bellows—Extension bellows and bellows components are more expensive than extension tubes, but these accessories are far more flexible and allow considerable room for continuous focusing and adjustment of the reproduction scale. Both bellows and extention tubes require precise focusing, exposure compensation, and some kind of ground-glass for focusing, such as is found in SLR's.

Before you invest in the bellows or extension tube type of close-up equipment, it is wise to check with the manufacturer of your camera and with a reputable camera store concerning its applicability and use with your camera.

Long Focal-Length Lenses—Although they are not really close-up equipment, these so-called telephoto lenses give a much larger image than standard (50mm) lenses and eliminate the necessity of working very close to the subject. If flowers are shot indoors, flash or strobe can be used with telephoto lenses, and the flowers will not wilt under the heat of the lamps. Outside, the telephoto allows you to isolate a single bloom, fill the entire image area with it, and at the same time selectively focus to drop out the background. Telephoto lenses are considerably more expensive than any other kind of close-up equipment, and they are bulkier (a tripod is required for anything over 200mm), but they come in sizes ranging from 85mm to 1200mm. These lenses are best used with SLR cameras, for on any other type of camera parallax is a problem; only the SLR's allow you to see exactly what the lens sees.

Mamiya twin lens reflexes with interchangeable lenses. Nikon F with Spiratone Telextender.

FOCUS AND VIEW

Of more importance than in any other kind of photography, focusing and viewfinding require the utmost care and attention when you are shooting close-ups. Focusing is critical because at extremely close range, the depth of field may run no more than a fraction of an inch (as shown in the table); if the subject is not in exact focus the result will be a fuzzy, unacceptable photo. Since the SLR's provide through-the-lens focusing, no matter what lens is being used, the problem is similar to other operations of the camera, that of precise focus and a steady camera. On all other types of camera, arrangements have to be made for sharp focusing.

When supplementary lenses are used with other than SLR cameras for close-up work, a simple way to focus is the string method. Since you know the distance at which your camera with close-up lens will be in perfect focus (from the table or the lens manufacturer's data sheet), you merely have to measure this distance accurately and shoot. Tape one end of unstretchable string to the camera lens mount, and at the other end tie a knot at the exact distance the camera will be in focus. For example: with 1+ and 3+ lenses in position, the knot would be tied at 10 inches. The string is held taut with the knot at the flower; then the string is dropped and the picture taken.

Poor focusing cost fine photo of daylily. Photographer shooting under poor lighting did not focus well enough to compensate for very short depth of field.

Focal frame attached to Kodak Automatic 35. White card is reflector to fill in shadows.

A tape measure can also be used, if compensation is made for the distance between the tape measure held to the camera and the lens mount. The procedure for using the tape measure is the same as that used for the string, except that the tape can be used for several lens combinations without the bother of changing it.

The other major problem confronting the photographer, when shooting flowers close up, is viewfinding. Here, again, with all cameras except the SLR's, the bugaboo of parallax appears. While it is a simple matter to tilt the camera upward a bit to compensate for the fact that on most cameras the viewfinder is above the lens, this method is inaccurate and usually unsatisfactory. For example, unless your camera has a special viewfinder that is parallax corrected, the top 1/4 will not appear on the film when a 3+ lens is used, the top 1/6 with a 2+ lens, and the top 1/8 with a 1+ lens.

A better solution to the viewing (parallax) problem, as well as the focusing problem, is the focal frame. These handy-dandy gadgets can either be bought at most camera stores or built at home. Simply made from tubular metal extending out from the camera to outline exactly the area in sharp focus, their main drawback is that each focal frame is made for use with a specific lens. This means a separate focal frame must be carried for each lens or combination of lenses. However, they are accurate and handy to use, giving an exact measure of the distance, height, and width of the area in focus.

77

Correct use of focus and depth of field keeps both foreground and background soft while maintaining sharp subject.

LIGHTING

A great many lighting possibilities are available to the photographer taking close-ups of flowers. Included in this list are daylight, flash (electronic and bulbs), photofloods, and reflectors. As with other forms of photography, where correct lighting can make or break a photo, close-up flower photography demands the utmost in special care and attention.

Daylight—There is some disagreement among experts concerning the use of clear sunlight for flower close-ups. Some say it is ideal, giving strong shadows that help to "pop out" the subject, full-color saturation, and greater definition. Others say it is less than ideal because the harsh shadows detract from the subject. These photographers say the best time to take flower close-ups outdoors is on a dull, overcast day, while the first group says that this kind of light gives a softer image and less definition. It all depends on what you are shooting and what you hope to get.

For just about the best shots of flowers using sunlight as the light source, take the pictures either early in the morning or toward late afternoon. At these times the shadows are longer and less harsh. and the sun, shining at an angle, gives the required light and enough shadow for modeling and detail. Reflectors can be used to give additional form to the flowers and fill in some deep shadows.

Electronic Flash—Without any doubt, flash, especially electronic flash, is the ideal light source when one is working close up with flowers. Electronic flash has a flash duration of about 1/1000 sec., eliminating the possibility of camera or subject movement; produces very little heat so it won't wilt the flowers; provides enough light close up for slow films exposed at small apertures; allows the photographer to use the same daylight film indoors and out; is inexpensive in the long run; and is extremely reliable.

Electronic flash does have one or two disadvantages, but these do not diminish its usefulness for close-up flower photography. One minor problem, when one uses electronic flash, is that focal plane cameras must be set at a slow speed, 1/50 sec., or only a portion of the film is exposed. Since flowers do little moving, except outside in a breeze, this problem is minimized by the very brief flash duration. The second problem, that of being unable to see the effects of the lighting arrangement before shooting, can be overcome through experience with the equipment and the usual bit of trial and error.

Malak. Lighting gives translucency to tulip and makes photo outstanding and not just another flower shot.

Strobe unit proved invaluable in capturing various stages of Germain's Ben Hur.

Electronic flash can be used successfully outdoors either as a fill-in source or as the primary light source, but it should be used with care. When you shoot close-ups with electronic flash outdoors, determine the exposure as if there were no sunlight. That is, determine the guide number (each film has a guide number for each different flash unit) and divide this by the distance to ascertain the f/number. The flash will provide enough light and will not be affected adversely by the sunlight.

For simple record shots, flash on the camera will assure you a photo every time. However, since the same lighting rules apply to close-up photography as to all other photography, the result will be quite flat. Flash off the camera, up and to the left, will give enough light and still allow for modeling and form without extremely harsh shadows.

Flashbulbs—Most of the discussion on electronic flash in close-up photography can be repeated for the use of flashbulbs. Although the flash duration of bulbs is considerably shorter than for electronic flash (1/50 versus 1/1000 sec.), this is usually not a problem. At any shutter speed of 1/50 or less, sufficient light will reach the film for complete exposure. Though flashbulbs still come in clear or blue, most films have now been improved so blue bulbs may be used with either black-and-white or color film. Check the film box or data sheet before using blue bulbs. Eventually all film will be made for use with only the blue flashbulbs.

Photofloods—The heat given off by photoflood lamps is a very severe disadvantage when they are used for close-up flower photography. One way they can be used, without wilting the subject, is through the use of a stand-in. That is, another flower is put into position and the lights are set up for shooting. After all the adjustments and changes in the lighting and the camera have been made and all is ready for shooting, the actual flower to be photographed replaces the stand-in. Even with this sort of system, the photographer must work with great speed, for almost any flower will start to droop as soon as the intense heat given off by these lamps hits them.

Spot lamps make fine substitutes for photoflood lamps. The light given off by the spot lamps is concentrated with the beam adjustable to hit only the area where light is required. Since the spot lamps can be adjusted to provide a light beam of specialized size and brightness at various distances from the subject, some of the heat problem can be minimized by concentrating the light and moving the lamp farther away from the flowers. One caution in using these lamps: Unlike photofloods, the spot lamps are extremely directional, so the harsh shadows should be softened with reflectors or other lights. A slide projector can be used in place of a spot lamp, but since the bulb may be damaged if the projector is used in any but a horizontal position, a mirror should be used for reflecting light onto the subject rather than using the projector itself in an unnatural position.

When you use photofloods, spots, or projectors as a light source, be sure to change to tungsten type film. If your camera is loaded with daylight film, a conversion filter can be used, but this is not quite as good as tungsten film without a filter.

Reflectors—These unofficial pieces of equipment are very often the unsung heroes of photographic lighting. Used for fill-in lighting and shadow reduction, reflectors can be made from white cardboard, aluminum covered cardboard, or concave mirrors, according to the kind and amount of light desired. In a pinch, even a clean, shiny cookie sheet can be used as a reflector. Shiny white cardboard will reflect more light than matte finish cardboard, but less than aluminum, with concave mirrors giving the most light reflectance and greatest light direction control.

It is important to use clean white board or colorless materials as reflectors when you shoot with color film, since any color on the reflector will be reflected to some degree onto the subject. For example, a light blue reflector, or background, will cool off the actual color of the subject. This is also true of surrounding areas when you shoot color outdoors—some amount of color will be reflected from surrounding foliage and plants onto the subject, tinting the true flower color

FILM

The ideal film for close-up photography would be a very fine-grain, high-definition, high-speed film. Since this combination is not available, film selection must be a compromise. Since high definition is the primary concern when close-ups are shot, a fine-grained, relatively slow film should be used. Kodachrome II and Panatomic X should do the required job admirably.

The other concern in choosing a film is, of course, the light source. Unless it is impossible, use the correct film for each different light source (daylight reversal color film with sunlight, tungsten type with photofloods, etc.). Using the correct film for the light source is considerably superior to using conversion filters.

Simple, almost never fail record shot of Can-Can petunia, Crossman Seed.

Calla lilies

CHAPTER VII

The Fun of Flowers Indoors

Flower photography is limited neither by weather nor by season; it is truly an all-year-round hobby. Often indoor flower photography is more satisfying and more satisfactory than outdoor. Indoors, a shooting session is not at the mercy of the elements. It is also true, however, that for the photographer there is nothing more pleasant than a beautiful day and the time to roam through the city, country, parks, or gardens, shooting away to his heart's content.

For those times of year and weather that do not permit such a photographic gambol, the easily controllable variables of indoor photography offer both an opportunity and a challenge. Indoors we needn't worry about a mischievous breeze suddenly ruining our composition, or wait for a big dark cloud to unblock our primary and only light source, or slowly seethe and simmer as person after person saunters slowly and unseeingly between us and our subject. Indoors we control the elements, not vice versa. That is, we can usually pick and choose, safe in the knowledge that everything will be as we want it when we are ready to shoot.

However, there are still a great many variables to be considered, and since most, if not all, can be controlled, the photographer should go down a checklist to insure that everything is in order.

SUBJECT

Imagination is just about the only limitation to selecting horticultural subjects for photographing indoors. Always available are the old favorites—house plants with shiny foliage or interestingly shaped leaves, or new plant varieties from Central and South America with huge exotic leaves or smaller, more delicate leaf patterns with iridescent undersides. In addition to these are the lately developed hybrids, which add splashes of white or color to their already beautifully shaped leaves. Also available are all the flowers and plant materials from cuttings and other gardens. With this almost total lack of limitation, the criteria for subject selection are simple: What is available? What do you like?

Full sized bonsai makes fine hobby as well as excellent photographic subject.

When house plants are prepared for photographing, the plants should be pruned and carefully examined so that only perfect leaves remain. The leaves should then be wiped with a soft cloth dampened with a small amount of lemon oil. Since the main pictorial attraction of house plants is their graceful and sometimes unusual lines, they should be further pruned to a pleasing shape and composition. A plant that has been nursed along for years on a window sill can often provide an interesting and eye-pleasing foliar composition. Just prior to getting the plant set up for the camera, check the soil. Often an unpleasant-looking residue collects on the top or sides of the container. If this appears, either mix the soil gently or cover it with potting soil or damp peat moss.

The preparation of flowers from an outside garden (to be photographed indoors) is no more complicated than the method listed above, but it does require more care and a bit more knowledge of flower stem types. When you cut flowers, do it either early in the morning or in the evening when it is cool. Just like people, plants tend to wilt and sag a bit during the heat of the day; therefore, if you must cut flowers at this time, rush them into a cool, dark spot, and allow considerable time for them to recover before arranging them for pictures.

86

Indoor-outdoor coleus by Park Seed.

To represent the flower on film as it was while growing, it is most important that the various flower types be cut according to stem requirements and that provisions be made for appropriate rejuvenation. Always cut flowers on a sufficiently long stem. All too often short stems are impossible to place in an arrangement. Once cut, protect the flower from bruising by carrying in a large box, one that allows the flowers to be spread out, not lying one atop the other.

CONDITIONING

Flowers must be conditioned and handled correctly if they are to look fresh and beautiful for the camera. To lengthen the time that a flower will look fresh and beautiful, determine the stem classification to which your flowers belong, and treat them accordingly. A discussion of these six classifications follows.

Woody stems—Flowers that grow on woody stems, *i.e.,* chrysanthemums, roses, stock, certain peonies, and lilacs, should have the cut end of the stalk battered with a hammer or the back end of your garden clippers before being set in a vase or arrangement. This type of plant absorbs water slowly, and the additional surfaces exposed through this fiber breakdown will allow for better water absorption and help keep the bloom fresh longer.

87

Hollow stems—Zinnias, delphiniums, dahlias, and other plants with hollow stems will keep well if the stems are carefully filled with water just prior to setting them into an arrangement. If they should sag after this treatment, protect the blossoms with tissue paper and dip the stem ends into several inches of boiling water. Keep them in the boiling water for about two minutes and then plunge them immediately into cold water. Let the stems remain in the cold water for as long as possible (overnight is excellent), and they should certainly be rejuvenated and fresh looking.

Bleeding plants—The liquid in the stems of some plants, such as poinsettias, poppies, and hollyhocks, bleeds when cut. Plants bleeding this milky sap require special attention if you want them to last long enough to be photographed. Immediately after cutting these flowers, out in the garden if possible, seal the cut ends by searing with a candle or cigarette lighter. After the bleeding has stopped, put the flowers in cold water.

Bulbous flowers—Gladioli, tulips, and narcissi are some of the flowers falling into this category. The faster these flowers are plunged into water, the longer they will last. The water should come up to the first open floret on a gladiolus stalk and to the flower head on tulips and other bulb flowers. When you cut these soft-stemmed flowers, use a sharp knife and cut at an angle, smoothly and quickly. Be sure that the slice is clean and the stalk has not been shredded.

Annuals—Immediate dunking into a pail of cold water is the order of the day for annuals such as marigolds and petunias. The pail of flowers should be kept in a cool, dark place for several hours before the blooms are arranged and photographed.

Flowers that need no water—Although flowers such as camelias, hibiscus, and orchids do not require that their stems be kept in water, it is a good idea to spray a mist of water over the blooms at least twice a day, to help keep them fresh and alive looking.

If, even after the conditioning indicated, the flowers start to droop, use the shock treatment of dipping the stems into boiling water and then cold water as suggested for hollow-stemmed plants. Be sure to protect the flowers with tissue paper during the boiling water portion of the treatment, or the steam will wilt the blossoms and all will be for naught.

In all cases, it is not a wise idea to try to squeeze in a shooting session if the flowers begin to droop. Instead, put the flowers into a vase in a cool, dark place and allow them to soak for several hours before attempting to rearrange them for shooting.

Conditioning chrysanthemums by smashing stem to allow rapid absorption when placed in water.

Also, before arranging them, trim off any lower leaves that might set in the water. Their removal will keep that water from becoming stagnant quickly and will also allow more water to reach the blooms.

In some cases, subject selection depends not so much on what the photographer likes, but on what the ultimate consumer likes. For personal shots, you shoot what you like, the way you like it. However, for pictures for garden clubs, photo clubs, or contests, you may have to change your thinking just a bit. For example, garden clubs are most interested in the specimen; therefore, extreme close-ups showing both the inside and outside of the flower are essential. The photo club is interested in an effective photograph, so use few flowers, arrange them interestingly, and make a dramatic shot. No matter whom your photographs are intended to please, always select your subject carefully and always cut your model flowers just before they have opened fully. Once cut and placed in water, the flowers will open to full size and yet still look fresh and beautiful.

BACKGROUNDS

As with all other types of photography, indoor flower photography requires compatibility of the elements making up the photo. They must not only be compatible, they must also add something to help complete the picture. For this reason, backgrounds must be carefully selected to add to the beauty or drama of the subject, but must not

Belgian begonias brought indoors

dominate or become overly obtrusive. That is, flowers are rarely shot in extreme low-key or against a black background. This would tend to overdramatize and make the finished photo too stark, rather than to suggest the grace, elegance, and light-heartedness usually associated with flowers.

The answer to the question of backgrounds is a set of cardboards, at least 20 X 30 inches, in various shades of gray, and several 30X 40-inch white boards. Other materials may also be adapted for backgrounds, such as cloth, wallpaper, grass cloth, matting, and bamboo screens. But remember, the key to success remains simplicity. Whatever material you choose for your background, your primary aim is to capture the delicate beauty of your subject, and this must never be overpowered by a heavily patterned background.

To further insure that the background stays in the background, and to reduce the possibility of confusing shadows, always be sure to set the subject far enough away from the background. There is no set rule for the distance of the subject from the background; just continue to move the plant container forward and backward until the shadows are softened as they fall from the subject onto the background. A photoflood lamp placed at the base of the background will also soften or entirely eliminate shadows; here again, trial and error is the best way to get pleasing results. Also, remember that the background can be diffused considerably by opening up the lens as wide as possible. Very sharp focusing on the subject will then be critical, but the background will be fuzzed out and will blend unobtrusively into the photo composition. As another extra to be considered, the photoflood can help change the gray value of your background, especially when a white cardboard is used. The farther away from the background it is, the darker it will appear, and vice versa.

It should be understood at this point that the simple, unadorned, white background is not necessarily the be-all and end-all for good indoor flower photography. Often a textured or patterned background can be quite effective. Also adding to the total composition of a flower photo can be pretty containers, figurines, added foliage, or other decorative material. While it is important not to overpower the subject or cause distractions from the central theme, it is equally important to realize that the flower or plant should not stand completely alone. As long as the additional material adds to the over-all effect, subtly and unobtrusively enhancing the whole tone, it can and should be used. Consider the total effect of the photo as you are setting it up and then light the photo to get maximum results.

Gourds too can be beautiful

X-15 marigolds by Ferry Morse

LIGHTING

To photograph flowers indoors the light can be daylight (coming through a window), daylight and artificial light (photoflood), or artificial light alone.

For daylight photography indoors, the best bet is a window with a northern exposure where the light comes in soft and bright for a period of time every day. Direct sunlight is not to be confused with brightness. Brightness will softly illuminate most parts of your flower arrangement with a minimum of distracting shadow, while direct sunlight will wash out certain colors and add dark, unattractive shadows to the photo. When you shoot indoors with daylight, place the subject in a position so the light from the window hits it at a 45-degree angle. This will usually mean that the flowers must be placed on or near the floor so the 45-degree lighting angle may be achieved. A reflector (one of the white cardboards or a board covered with aluminum foil) is used to reflect some of the light back onto the subject and, in so doing, softens many very dark areas. Lighting this way will bring out all flower details, snap out the stems and leaves, and keep everything from blending into the background.

Though not recommended as general or good practice, daylight and artificial light can be used together when black-and-white film is shot indoors. Color film should never be shot with more than a single type of light. When both daylight and photofloods are used, extra care must be taken with the exposure meter reading, since the tendency is for incorrect readings when more than one type of light is in use.

However, daylight and photofloods, when used carefully and correctly together, can give very soft, pleasing results. To best achieve the correct blend of the two different kinds of light, it is wise to use the daylight as if it were the only light source being used, and to use the photofloods to light the background or provide highlights. Remember, when you use photofloods, to be completely set up, focused, etc., before turning them on, keeping them on only as long as is absolutely necessary. If they are left on too long, the heat generated by these lights will wilt the flowers.

When you use artificial light in the form of photofloods as the sole light source for your exposure, you are giving yourself the opportunity to paint the composition with light. The classic arrangement or lighting pattern consists of a key light placed 45 degrees from the camera lens axis, a diffused light placed low and close to the camera (off to the right a bit), a subject light placed close to and above the flowers to highlight and remove shadows, and a fourth light aimed from the bottom of the background to the top to eliminate harsh shadows that might fall on the background.

Once the classical pattern has been set up, begin experimenting with the lights so as to best show off the subject and set a mood, thereby enhancing the resultant photograph. Continue to move the lights up, down, and sideways until exactly the right combination has been achieved. When you have done this, it is a good idea (and one that will save much time and trouble) to make a quick diagram of the layout for future reference. Do not forget to use reflectors as required with any lighting layout you might choose.

Flash guns and strobe units can be used successfully for flower photography, each having the added feature of no heat—the light is flashed for a split second with no heat given off to wilt the subject. Much the same setup should be used for flash or strobe as is used for photofloods. To synchronize the auxiliary units to the master unit, slave units that are automatically tripped by the light from the master unit should be used.

COMPOSITION

Virtually all of the composition of indoor flower photography falls into the category of flower arrangement, the subject of the next chapter. There are, however, several items of interest that should be mentioned here.

First and foremost is the idea that the best composition is the least composition. Simplicity is the byword, and if this is set as a goal when flower photos are composed, the photos will be able to stand on their own, with the subject's beauty, line, and form dominating. All this occurs without the deliberate and often obvious attempt at composition.

A second thought to consider when you compose flower photos indoors is that nature knows best, and flowers should be composed within a format that most closely approximates actual growth conditions. Also, never feel that the more flowers one can cram into a photo, the better it will be. Often, a single blossom is sufficient, although most times two or more are required to make the photo pleasing and lifelike.

Another item of interest is that flowers are interesting, if not beautiful, at each and every phase of development. Serious thought should therefore be given to which phase you want to photograph. For example, the rose offers beauty all through its growth cycle: from foliage to bud, to opening bud, to bloom, to fully open bloom.

Ornamental corn by Park used as a bouquet.

Light yellow Sunburst in Grandiflora class by Pan American Seed Co.

Any one alone, or a few in combination, can provide a magnificent photograph.

A parting thought on this short discussion of composition is a note that covers all photographic composition, but seems to apply especially to flower photography. Use your own taste, good sense, and personal preference to determine good composition. If you can honestly say your photo is pleasant to look at, uncomplicated, and simply arranged to make viewing easy, then your composition, and most likely your photo as well, is better than average. Develop this sense of composition so it becomes natural for you to have well-composed photos. Well-composed photos are better photos.

DICK WHITTINGTON

Prize winning carnation arrangement.

CHAPTER VIII

Photography and Flower Arranging

Throughout most of history, flower arranging has been a recognized and flourishing art form. The civilizations of the ancient Egyptians, and later of the Persians, Greeks, Romans, and Goths, all show evidences of the importance of the beauty of floral arrangements to their cultures. This importance continues to the present day, when flower arrangements play an integral part in bringing some of nature's beauty into our everyday lives. To go a step further, we form a partnership between a very old and a very new art form when we photograph flower arrangements.

While it is not our intention to try to teach the photographer, or seduce him into an entirely new hobby, it is important that he know the basics of this art form. The knowledge will stand him in good stead for photographing arrangements. It should also allow him to make simple arrangements from his flowers and thus get double pleasure. Besides, someone has to make the arrangements for you to photograph, and who knows better what you want than you!

FLOWERS AND PLANTS

The flowers for your arrangements can come from any or all of four places: your own garden, a commercial grower or greenhouse, a florist, or the flower market in your city. The wisest thing is to pick and choose from each, naturally looking first to your own garden. During the seasons when your garden cannot supply your needs, fresh-cut flowers can be obtained in steady profusion from the other sources. The variety of flowers available at most times of the year is almost unlimited. Anything needed quickly and desperately can usually be shipped from other parts of the country if it is unavailable where you live. For your arrangements you will need the basic flowers, foliage, and shrubs, plus whatever you feel necessary for an over-all effect.

97

When you select plant material for your arrangement, be sure it suits the mood you wish to set: Lilies suggest elegance and the columbine, delicacy; sheer exquisite beauty is always the rose. Combine your blossoms in a harmonious design and you will indeed have created a piece worth preserving on film. If you keep your eyes open to the variety of color, shape, and environment taking place in nature, many ideas and materials will make themselves obvious and available to your camera.

Unless this new hobby does indeed attract you and you plan to enter your arrangements in flower shows, most of your efforts will be for home and camera. Since there are really no rules by which you *must* be governed, your choice of materials, containers, backgrounds, etc., will be governed by what you like and what you think looks good.

CONTAINERS

Though not the center of attention, the container holding the arrangement can make or break the entire effort. Almost anything that will hold a bit of water, or hold a can that will hold water, can be used successfully. Of prime importance is that the container suit the arrangement and vice versa.

Scabrosa by Ferry Morse in varying stages of development.

98

Containers suitable for flower arranging come from all over the world, can cost pennies or thousands of dollars, and appear in every imaginable color, size, shape, and surface quality. In selecting a container for a particular arrangement, we must take these four physical determinants into consideration and relate them singly and in combination to the flowers to be placed in the container.

Color—For color photography, even more than for black-and-white, the container should be as neutral in color as possible so as not to detract from the flowers. The best colors, then, are white, tan, gray, black, and the soft pastels. There is generally enough color in the arrangement without adding more through the use of a colored container. In black-and-white photography any color container may be used as long as the gray tone representing the color does not overpower the gray tones of the flowers. Metal containers are fine as long as they don't have a high shine that will bounce back into the camera lens. Glass containers can also be used, but they should not be transparent—the mess of jumbled stalks and stems below the water line can ruin the most magnificent arrangement.

Size—The size of the container is governed, obviously, by the size and kind of flower arrangement planned. To be certain that the flowers will be dominant, a rule of thumb is that the arrangement should be one and one-half times as tall as the container. Similarly, common sense and good judgment should prevail in indicating when a container is too small and in danger of being overturned by a top-heavy arrangement. When you select a container on the basis of size, be certain that it is in proportion to the arrangement in all dimensions, not only in height. There should be a balance achieved between the complete arrangement and the over-all size of the container, if maximum design and beauty are to be achieved.

Shape—Included in the list of shapes for containers are urns, beakers, cylinders, vases, bottles, gourds, and virtually all other imaginable shapes. As is the case for the other physical characteristics of containers, the shape must suit the arrangement. If the flowers selected for the arrangement are tall and straight (such as gladiolus stalks), a good container would be one that is tall and slender with simple, clean lines. If, however, the flowers to be arranged are to be curved within a design, a container with soft curves complementing the curve of the floral design can be used. As with everything else in flower arranging, the containers must be of a shape that will enhance, never detract from, the center of importance, the flowers.

Surface Quality—Two criteria must be observed when containers

Cosmos arrangement is simple yet elegant.

are selected on the basis of surface quality: (1) Does the surface quality go with the kind of flowers to be used? (2) Does the quality of the container fit into its surroundings? If the flowers to be used are heavy or coarse, the container must balance them; it must be sturdy and substantial looking, but not overpowering. Similarly, dainty, delicate flowers belong in dainty, delicate containers. For the purposes of photographing an arrangement, as long as the background is either clean or extremely simple, a patterned or textured container is no problem. However, with any sort of background pattern, the container must have no pattern and little texture, and must be clean-lined and simple. If the arranger sticks to simplicity and clean lines, he is increasing his chances of success manyfold.

The photographer—flower arranger should keep all these things in mind when making his selection—color, size, shape, and surface quality. Then, when he has selected the container he believes is best for his arrangement, he must determine if it will photograph well. For example, glass containers can't be shot head-on; the flash must be off the camera. Silver containers should be "dimmed" with a spray compound so the light doesn't bounce, and other containers made of materials that will pick up reflections, photograph spottily, or otherwise be unsuitable for photographing must be avoided. A good test for eliminating such problems is to set up the container, without flowers, and view it under the photoflood lights just as it would be when formally arranged for the camera. In this way any possible problems should show up before the damage is irreparable.

OTHER NECESSITIES

The two most important parts of any floral arrangement, the flowers and the containers, have already been discussed. There remains but one more class of equipment to be noted here—the items required to shape, twist, or hold the arrangement in place.

Holders—Of the hundred different holders on the market, probably the best, or at least the most popular, are the needle-point types. These heavy holders, when placed at the bottom of the container, maintain the position in which the flowers are impaled. Some of the other holders available include mesh (useful to brace flowers in a container), bird cages (especially good for table arrangements, since they allow flowers to be stuck in at all angles), hairpin (good to hold and anchor heavy flowers), and clustered leaf type (can be used singly or attached to others for a strong, useful holder).

John F. Kennedy rose arrangement.

If these holders are not available and you want an on-the-spot arrangement for shooting, several household items can be used on an emergency basis. These include sand (packed into the container and dampened a bit), a potato (slice off the bottom so it lies flat), fish-tank gravel, chicken wire (crumpled and made into a rough ball), evergreen branches (stuff them into the container vertically, then insert the flowers), and many other items that will make themselves obvious to you.

To anchor the manufactured variety of flower holders in place, clay or calk can be used. One important word of caution: Do not use clay or calk in a silver container; they cause irreparable damage. To hide the holders, bits of pretty crushed glass, pebbles, tiny stones, or colored gravel can be used.

Miscellaneous—Some other items that will be of valuable assistance to the photographer when he arranges his flowers are sharp shears, various kinds of wire, and green sticks. Sharp shears are a necessity because they cut most stems quickly and with a clean, neat cut. Dull shears will shred or smash the stem and, as explained more fully in the section on preparing flowers for arrangements, the flower will not last as long. Various kinds of wire are available which, when wrapped around the stem, will allow you to bend the flower into whatever curve or position you require. They may be used in similar fashion,

BLUE RIBBON FLOWER HOLDER CO.

by taping wire to the leaf underside, for positioning the leaves. Green sticks may be used to lengthen short stems (wire the two together, green stick below flower stem), to make dried-out material easier to bend, or as a support for certain soft-stemmed flowers.

There are a great many other items that can be included in the complete bag-of-tricks of the flower arranger: tin snips (to cut wire mesh), paring knife (to cut clay), pins, hammer (to smash stems), awl (to make holes), and battery syringe (for watering). However, for the photographer setting up such an arrangement for the camera, all these things are not necessities, and he will probably come up with his own expedients to get the job done—the job being, of course, to design and execute an arrangement of horticultural materials that will result in a beautiful arrangement and an equally beautiful photograph.

DESIGN

So the photographer can prepare a truly professional looking arrangement, he should know some of the basics of flower arrangement design. There are, of course, many full-length books devoted to this subject. However, for our purposes a short explanation should suffice, and any photographer desiring to further his knowledge in the area can easily do so.

The design of a flower arrangement should always follow a carefully thought-out plan, governed by the materials selected. Whatever materials, containers, and locations have been chosen, the finished piece should blend all the elements into one unified design. This design should be: simple, reducing the possibility of distractions; in accord with its surroundings, and within itself; beautiful for all who look at it; and expressive of your feelings at that time.

Design Elements—To best achieve the simplicity, beauty, harmony, and expression of good design, the photographer–arranger must next shift his attention to the basic elements of design. At the start, he should determine to which of the basic patterns his flowers, containers, etc., are best suited: triangle, rectangle, Hogarth curve (S-curve), circle, square, fan, and L-shape. In all probability it will be easier to work with the first four patterns, since these are the most commonly used.

Next, the photographer should determine the line of the arrangement. It indicates the line or path the eye takes getting from one point of interest to another. The focal area, or the center of interest, is the

Japanese inspired chrysanthemum arrangement.

place for the most outstanding part of the arrangement. The other elements in the arrangement are subservient to this focal area, but lead the eye, through the use of color, size, weight, etc., from the outer edges of the arrangement to and through the focal area and on to the fringe areas.

The over-all color arrangement is another of the design elements lending itself to the proper creation of the total picture. Colors should be used carefully and with an eye to what the finished product will look like with regard to color blending. The design can call for the use of complementary colors, monochromes, or if you are quite sure of what you are doing, colors that might appear to clash. No matter what colors are used, they must be considered as part of the design, not merely as colorful elements standing on their own.

Other design elements to be considered when an arrangement is planned and executed are similar to those used to select the proper container—shape or form, and surface quality or texture. As mentioned, all of the elements must be blended according to an over-all plan to create a beautiful, artistic arrangement. To achieve this total effect, principles of design are incorporated. These principles—balance, contrast, scale, proportion, repetition, rhythm, and dominance—require little explanation. Most mean exactly what they would seem to mean, and are important because they correctly mold the various elements into an eye-pleasing and camera-pleasing composition. Of special interest and importance are balance, contrast, and rhythm.

Balance—If we use an imaginary central axis as a dividing line, flower arrangements can be determined to have symmetrical or asymmetrical balance. In symmetrical balance, both sides of the arrangement are even in the amount and kind of material used. Asymmetrical balance sees the use of unequal amounts, arranged unequally to give the visual effect of over-all balance.

Contrast—Variety is the spice of flower arrangement as well as of life. Simple internal contrasts will not only assure variety, they will also arouse interest and keep the arrangement from becoming stagnant.

Rhythm—A smooth, gentle movement is essential to each arrangement. The smooth flow of line, color, and the direction of the arrangement will allow the viewer to see and enjoy this art form without disconcerting, mood-shattering breaks.

PHOTOGRAPHING ARRANGEMENTS

Although the two art forms seem made for each other, many problems occur when flowers and flower arrangements are captured on film. For example, the entire balance of the arrangement can be thrown completely out of kilter merely by the use of black-and-white film, by a single light in the wrong place, or by the camera being too high or too low.

As a result, it is important for the photographer to see before he shoots. He must see his subject, the arrangement, as if he were the camera, remembering that the camera will see all flaws and record them exactly as seen. Obviously, this is the place for a Polaroid camera. You can shoot the photo with the Polaroid and within 10 seconds for black-and-white, or 60 seconds for color, you have a finished photo to check. Since the Polaroid gives a photographic print, anything that might be wrong with your final print will appear, and can be corrected quickly and easily while the arrangement and equipment are still in place. An examination of some of the problems that may be encountered merit inclusion in this chapter.

As noted in Chapter IV, one of the most difficult parts of flower photography in black-and-white is the realization that the result will be in neither black-and-white nor color, but rather in shades of gray. Arrangements are especially susceptible to this problem, for within a perfectly balanced arrangement, a dominant flower color turns a dull gray or two different colored flowers reproduce the same shade of gray.

Another problem occurs as a result of the angle of the camera in relation to the arrangement. If the camera is held too high or too low, the arrangement becomes, on film, either too heavy or too squat. Similarly, the plane of the arrangement can be the cause of problems of perspective. A flower tipped a bit forward of the center line of the arrangement will dominate other flowers of the same size farther back in the arrangement.

Lighting and lights can also cause many problems when flower arrangements are photographed. For example, lights can flatten out the subject, point up holes or other errors in the arrangement, or cast shadows that can change the entire appearance of the arrangement.

The solution to these problems is not simple. It is, instead, a painstaking exercise in seeing, coupled with experience and liberally sprinkled with trial-and-error attempts. The photographer must learn to see his subject in the same manner as the camera sees it. Since the

FERRY-MORSE SEED CO.

Cherry tart petunias

107

Seashell containered arrangement

dimension of depth is greatly limited on film, the photographer should work, either himself or with the arranger, expecting this loss of dimension, and design the composition accordingly. If changes in the arrangement cannot be made, then the lights and the camera must be adjusted to compensate.

Lighting should be planned with each specific arrangement in mind. Since each arrangement is different, the problems will vary, and so must the lighting. Whereas a light from each side and on the background is usually enough, certain arrangements can be helped by additional lights. Backlighting, though often hard to control, is one way to give a third-dimensional effect to the subject.

Many of the problems in photographing flower arrangements can be avoided if they are taken into consideration when the arrangement is being designed, when the background is selected, when the lights are set up, and when the camera is positioned. Others can be seen in the viewfinder, especially when one works with a view camera or an SLR, and can be remedied on the spot. Still others can only be fixed after you have seen the goof on film. If a Polaroid is available, use it. If not, take many shots. Just as bracketing can be of immeasurable help in making sure of exposure, it can help here. Bracketing, in this case, is not concerned so much with exposure as with over-all composition. Take several pictures with lights and camera in a fixed position, and then make some small adjustments in each, shooting after each change; you will thereby greatly increase the possibility of truly fine flower arrangement photographs.

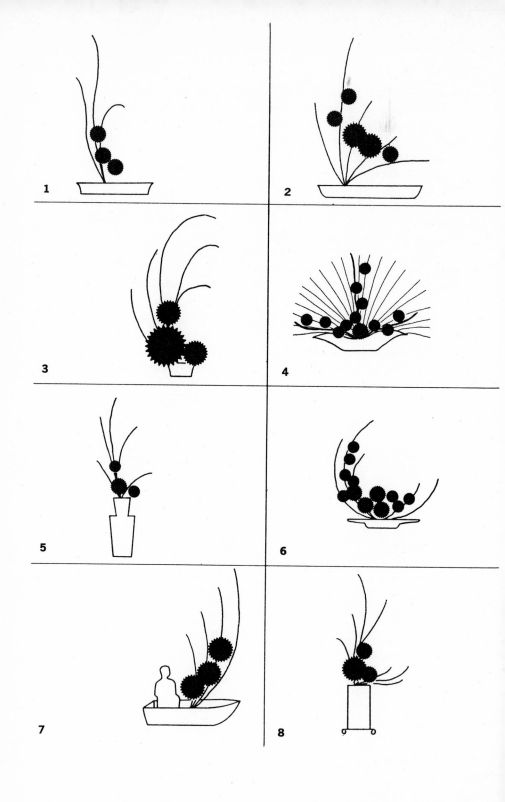

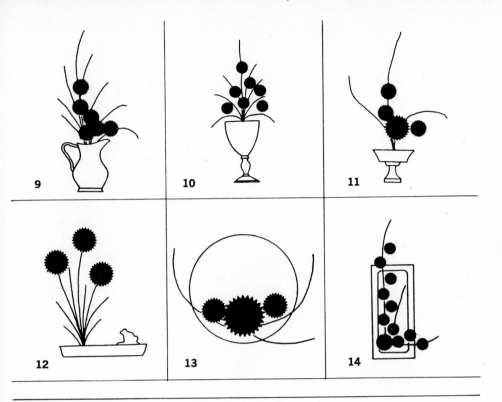

9
10
11
12
13
14

Flowers and foliages may be divided into two main types: lineal and solid. Use the line materials to form the outline or framework of your design. Group the solid flowers towards the center to create a focal point. Additional foliage and smaller flowers may be used to fill in the background, cover the mechanics and add weight to the lower part of the design.

1. Tall vertical design of snapdragons, carnations and salal.
2. Triangular design of forsythia, daffodils and salal leaves.
3. Curvilinear design of spiral eucalyptus, carnations and galax.
4. Fan design of one palmetto leaf and three stalks of gladioli.
5. High triangular design of roses, red leaf, huckleberry and galax.
6. Crescent design of Scotch broom, pompons and salal.
7. Triangular, sail-shaped design of pussy willow and tulips.
8. L-shaped design of pussy willow, iris and leucothoe foliage.
9. Pitcher design with Scotch broom, pussy willow, tulips and galax.
10. Traditional symmetrical triangle design of juniper and roses.
11. Three-line design of forced cherry branches, iris and galax foliage.
12. Naturalistic design of three Dutch iris, Baker fern and moss.
13. Top view of crescent table design of carnations and Baker fern.
14. Top view of triangular table design of gladioli and salal.

Malak. Magnificent Marianne Greigii tulip.

CHAPTER IX

Flower Shows and Exhibitions

If the number of cameras seen at flower shows and exhibitions is any indication, most flower lovers are photographers, and vice versa. Whether or not this is actually true, the flower shows and exhibitions offer fantastic opportunities for the flower lover and photographer to see and shoot. For there are usually available the latest horticultural varieties, prize-winning floral arrangements, great masses of varied colors, and almost everything else to make a virtual photographic paradise.

Unfortunately, unless some preplanning is done, this paradise can easily turn into a nightmare of frustration and wasted effort for the photographer. Part of the preplanning should include your personal photographic purpose at the show: a series of pretty pictures for showing when few real flowers are growing, a photographic notebook of new varieties, a cataloguing of the flowers and ideas you want for your garden, or a tourist's-eye view of a wonderful exhibition or show.

Although the kind of picture you take will reflect your ultimate goal, many of the ground rules for successful flower show and exhibition photography are the same and should be mentioned in the hope of possibly preventing one or more fiascos the next time.

One of the best suggestions for the photographer serious about getting good photographs at a flower show, is to arrive at a time when it is least crowded. This seems to occur pretty regularly three times a day: immediately after opening, at lunchtime, and at dinnertime. Therefore, try to attend during one of these times; the crowds will be smaller and the photographing easier. Of the three off-times, dinnertime, from about 5 to 7 P.M., seems to be the lightest on crowds. However, since your time of limited crowds is not always at your personal convenience, preplan, know what you want to shoot, and have all your equipment ready to go—make sure everything is available and ready to use.

Another item in the preplanning department is to be sure to have enough of everything, such as film and flashbulbs. If you are shooting black-and-white film, have plenty of fast film such as Tri-X, and the usually good available light will be sufficient. For color work, your best bet is either flash or strobe. Therefore, along with an adequate supply of film, make sure you have plenty of bulbs if not a well-charged strobe unit. To cut down on the bulkiness of several cartons of film (in your jacket pocket, gadget bag, or wife's handbag), remove the film cans from the carton and tape them securely to your camera's carrying strap. Bulbs, however, are best kept in their cardboard carrying sleeves.

As far as equipment is concerned, it is best to travel light, but not so light that you miss shots because of lack of equipment. You should certainly be able to manage excellently with the following equipment: tripod, flash or strobe, lens shade, and telephoto or close-up lenses. Above all, make sure everything is in proper working order.

Many flower shows prefer that tripods not be used in the exhibition halls because of the danger of someone tripping over the extended legs. If you run into this situation, try to rest your camera on anything that is available and steady. Any post, ledge, or other support will serve your purpose, and special care should then be exercised to assure smooth release of the shutter.

Be sure to bring along some sort of material or cardboard that will be suitable for use as a background if you are seeking special, professional-looking shots. Many of your very best shots taken at a show will be of one or two perfect blooms isolated from the great mass of flowers. For black-and-white shooting, two cardboards, one white and light gray and the other white and a darker gray, should do the trick admirably. While one gray board is used as a background, the white side of the second sheet can be used as a reflector to fill in shadows. For color shooting, large sheets of colored board, preferably pastel colors of pink and blue, should be used. Cloth can also be used as a background; since it can be folded it is considerably easier and more convenient to carry. However, be careful to select a fabric that does not wrinkle too badly, and throw the background out of focus when you shoot so any wrinkles that exist will not show.

As noted, the kind of pictures you take at the flower and garden shows will be determined by the ultimate use of the photos. If your aim is pretty pictures and lots of color, a variety of long, medium, and close-up shots should be taken. The long shots will give you the massed colors and the general growing arrangement of the flowers. These long shots are best taken from high above the plants. A chair or ladder will get you high enough above the display to give you a good over-all view. Incidentally, if you look as if you know what you are doing, and perhaps even have an assistant holding a second flash unit or strobelight, most people will stay out of the way while you take your picture. The key to success here is to be quick to set up and to look as efficient as possible.

Medium shots will give you pretty pictures to show, and are taken quickly and easily. Standing at ground level, find something with which to frame your picture. In many of the gardens set up at shows, a tree, fence, or arbor is included and would make a wonderful frame.

Close-ups, often of a single beautiful bloom, are perhaps the easiest of all to take from the standpoint of crowds. Since they must of necessity be taken at quite close range, no one can get between the camera and the plant.

Close-ups have been discussed earlier, but a few items should be noted here. A good rule of thumb to follow is that every long or medium shot should offer the possibility of at least six to ten close-ups. Every angle around the bloom is different and presents a fresh aspect for your camera. So, while the long shot will give you an over-all look at the planting, the close-ups will give you a detailed look and will truly complete the picture.

Another point to remember is one concerning the close-up use of flash or strobe. At extremely close range, the odds are the photo will be badly overexposed if either one is used. To combat this, a white

Candytuft by Crossman Seed

Prize winning hyacinths

handkerchief should be hung over the flash gun when one shoots from 3 feet away, and a double layer used for a distance of less than 3 feet. Some flash or strobe manufacturers supply a plastic cap to fit over the unit to help diffuse the light at such times. Whichever you use, remember that all close-up shots using flash or strobe will be ruined by overexposure, should you forget.

If you are using your camera at the flower show in place of a notebook, your best bet is close-ups. Most shows use markers of one sort or another to indicate the variety and often the grower. For the purposes of your camera notebook, a close-up shot of a new variety with the name of the maker clearly visible is ideal. A secondary shot should be taken of the over-all display to indicate the growing characteristics of the plants and how they can best be grouped for maximum effectiveness and beauty. Speaking of markers—like everything else, sometimes they are good and sometimes they are in the way. Very often the appearance of a marker in your picture will ruin the over-all effect. Therefore, if possible, carefully remove the marker from the ground, take your picture, and replace it immediately. Most often this will cause little or no stir, and will solve your problem. If there is an objection from the management, your only alternative is to try to find an angle at which the marker does not show.

For your tourist's-eye view of a flower show or exhibition, and for many fine flower photos, include people. But don't just plunk someone down in front of some flowers, staring straight into the camera lens. Instead, use your imagination and try to achieve a measure of naturalness between the people and the flowers. Have the people doing something. Smelling, looking, or touching are quite natural actions for a person who is admiring a group of flowers. This will probably mean that your subject cannot face the camera directly, but most will agree that a shot of a person in action is much better than a staring match between subject and camera.

Another reason to use a person in action when you photograph flowers is to determine the relative size and height of some plant. Just as component manufacturers often place a coin next to a miniature component, you are placing the relatively recognizable size of a person or a person's hand near a flower, showing height and bloom size.

Many of the photos you will get at flower shows and exhibitions will be well worth enlarging, framing, and even hanging in your home. While it is not so critical with black-and-white enlargements, it is not a good idea to blow up color photos larger than the actual size of the real flower. Actual-size color photos of flowers can be beautiful and extremely decorative in the home, but oversized shots can too easily look garish and are no longer pretty.

The horticultural shows held throughout the country offer unbeatable opportunities for the photographer. Here, everything is at its best, and so must be the photographer. With a bit of preplanning and a basic knowledge of his subject, the flower photographer can take beautiful flower photos and have a ball while doing it.

Dianthus

Seashell containered arrangement

Formal rose garden at United Nations.

CHAPTER X

Garden Photography

Few subjects are as disappointing when viewed on film as well filled, blooming gardens. To the eye, the masses of colors, and the variety of blooms, are pretty. Recorded on film, especially black and white film, this same view is often a complete flop. The beauty of the flowers, trees, and foliage becomes something considerably less than that—a mass (or perhaps mess would be a better word) of multi-colored blobs on color film, and dull, uninteresting globs of gray or black on black and white film.

The first step toward good garden photography is to define the term. For our purposes, garden photography will be considered to be that part of photography that records groups of growing things, either cultivated or wild, as opposed to the close-up of a single subject. Garden photography, then, includes shrubs, trees, vegetables and plant groupings in formal and informal settings.

Naturally, one good close-up is often worth a great many wide-angle shots. But, this is side-stepping our definition and the problem at hand. A massed grouping of magnificent white parrot tulips is beautiful to see, but murder to photograph. While a close-up would be easy and effective, it still leaves the remainder of the garden to be photographed.

EXAMINE YOUR SUBJECT

As is generally the case in other areas of photography, the best way to get good results is to know your subject. Since most gardens, trees and shrub groupings are quite large, the logical first step is to walk around and look at the potential subject. Don't look at it through the camera viewfinder . . . just look at your subject as you would an oil painting . . . as a piece of natural art. Seek out the most interesting features and visualize how they will look and reproduce in a photograph.

It is at this point in garden photography that good photos are made . . . they don't just happen. With the most interesting or important features of the garden in mind, start to make sure that these will take "center stage" in your finished shot. Do not attempt to include everything in your field of vision in a single shot. If you do, you most probably will end up with a landscape type of photo rather than a garden photo. Select a camera position that will give you an interesting angle on the garden, while including only what you want, maintaining some semblance of perspective, and capturing the subject in a normal, natural looking manner.

COMPOSITION

There are several hints and suggestions that should come in handy when preparing a garden for photographing. Many flowers do not grow in exactly the position or attitude that makes for a good photo, so help them to become more photogenic. For example, daffodils have often been known to turn their backs on the camera. A few bits of florist's wire and some cardboard can be used to make them pay attention. Chrysanthemums generally grow in a scattered, unappealing mess. Bunch them together with wire or string to get a massed color effect. Cockscomb grows in a beautiful, velvety red . . . but they grow singly. A bit of quick transplanting will give you a magnificent picture. If transplanting sounds like a bit too much trouble, flowers such as marigolds can be cut the day before, conditioned, stuck into the ground for the photo, then brought into the house as cut flowers. By placing the cut or transplanted flowers into carefully selected areas, they can be used for accent, interest or to round out and fill in any bare spots.

Another very important consideration when shooting gardens is the surroundings. The soil and the lawn around the garden beds have the same relationship as a frame has to a picture. It is the same as getting all dressed up in a new suit and wearing old shoes that need a shine. It spoils the picture! While it may begin to seem that the preparation for the photo takes an inordinately long time, rest assured that the time is well spent. The grass surrounding the garden should be freshly clipped to a height that is neither too tall nor too short. The soil in the garden should be deep brown, recently turned, and moist. Stones or dropped flower petals should be picked up to avoid white spots on the print. It is very important that extra care be taken to "see" a great variety of imperfections, and remove them before the picture is taken. Unfortunately, what often appears to be "nothing" to the eye, sticks out like a sore thumb in a photo.

Another good idea to consider when setting up a garden photo is the use of water as an assistant. After everything is in position and ready to be shot, water the area well, using a sprinkler head attached

Malak. Solid black is best background for this poppy.

to the hose. This kind of watering will wash any dirt or dust from the petals and leaves, remove residue of insecticide sprayings, make the foliage look sharp and crisp, and turn the soil a rich, dark brown, perfect as a contrast to the flowers and leaves.

Incidentally, speaking of watering, an interesting thought is that just about the best time to take garden photos is soon after a spring or summer rainstorm. The rainstorm will clear the atmosphere and wet everything down, increasing the contrast between the flowers, foliage and background, and at the same time, greatly improve the color saturation of the petals.

Getting back to garden photo composition, once you have manicured the surrounding area, filled in the gaps in the planting, and selected the correct camera position, the next consideration should be the background. A fine, almost always available background is the blue sky. Position your camera so you are shooting up from a low angle toward the sky, with the subject occupying the lower two-thirds of the photo and the sky filling in the remaining third. Very often it will be necessary to move the tall stalks of such flowers as hollyhocks so they are clear of any distracting influence and stand clear before the sky background. Wire or string, placed out of camera range, can be used to move the flower stalks to a clear position.

Pan American Seed's appleblossom petunia in a natural environment.

When shooting gardens in black and white the additional problem of monochromatic rendering must be considered. While much of the information on this subject is contained in the chapter on black and white films, it is appropriate to note here that proper color correction can mean the difference between a good and a poor garden photo. Because many colors are rendered almost the same tone of gray on panchromatic film (this is the most widely used black and white film), a scene with varicolored flowers looks lovely to the eye in color but is totally lackluster on black and white. The use of a yellow filter will help immeasurably, since it will improve the rendition of reds and yellows, darken the blue sky and "pop-out" the clouds. It should become obvious that the sharp, clearly defined results achieved using the yellow filter are far superior to the drab, massed grays resulting when no filter is used.

The best kind of lighting for garden photography is natural and comes strongly from either the back or side. While this kind of lighting will result in considerable shadows, this can be offset through the use of fill-in flash or reflectors, and the resultant color saturation is well worth the effort. Of course, fill-in illumination can only be applied to relatively small garden areas, so, if the subject is quite large,

Small corner of a garden makes pleasing photo.

123

discretion must be used to determine the kind of lighting available that will give the best color saturation while maintaining proper definition of texture and flower modeling.

DEPTH OF FIELD

Depth of field is just about the last major consideration when setting up to take garden photos. Very often great depth of field is required to keep many important elements in the photo in sharp focus. This then means that slow shutter speeds and small apertures are the order of the day—so the time of day for shooting the garden photos should be selected with a view toward all the variables present. Probably the best time to shoot these photos is early in the morning. At this time, the atmosphere is clear, there is usually little breeze, and the shutter and diaphragm settings can be made suitable to getting the best possible shots.

Throughout, we have spoken of garden and flower photos and photography in terms of almost optimum conditions. Though to a great extent most flower and garden photos will be taken during the good weather months of spring and summer, the remainder of the year should not be dismissed as "no time to take pictures outdoors." Nothing is further from the truth. Both fall and winter offer unmatchable opportunities for beautiful and dramatic photos of trees, leaves and even gardens.

Some of the most magnificent photos in stark black and white, or even occasionally in color, are available when the trees are covered with snow or ice. Here again, the best photos can be taken either very early or very late in the day, when the low angle of the light combined with side or backlighting will produce dramatic effects without the harsh shadows usual at other times of day.

Fall too offers what amounts to a photographer's paradise, for many trees show a display of color unmatched even by the beauty of spring and summer.

The great difference in color between the spring-summer and fall-winter seasons is one of degree. In the spring-summer part of the year, the colors are usually pastel and beautiful in a serene sort of way. The fall-winter colors are deeper, richer and more riotous, and must be properly treated so as to make the best possible use of their boldness. Once again, early or late in the day shooting combined with back or side lighting and judicious use of filters should result in memorable photographs.

Rose after rainstorm.

The all-encompassing photos of gardens or pastoral scenes can be beautiful and quite eye-catching, but they must be preplanned and correctly set up. A quick snapshot of a garden, flower bed, orchard or planting will result in nothing more or less than a snapshot. To get good garden photos, select, compose, light, expose and, above all . . . SEE.

Index